Φορτεανσ Υνϖειλεδ: Φαμιλψ ςαυλτ οφ Συπερνατυραλ ανδ Παρανορμαλ

Forteans Unveiled

Family Vault of Supernatural and Paranormal

MC LORBIECKE

Μαριτα Χηριστινε Λορβιεχκε

Copyright © 2023 Author Name

All rights reserved.

ISBN: 979-8-9893391-0-5

Φορτεανσ Υνϖειλεδ: Φαμιλψ ςαυλτ οφ Συπερνατυραλ ανδ Παρανορμαλ

Μαριτα Χηριστινε Λορβιεχκε

DEDICATION

Like each one, this book is dedicated to my beloved husband, twin flame, and soul mate, John D. Lorbiecke, for always supporting me. To Anton for being the best supporter of whom a writer could dream. To my in-laws, John and Josie Lorbiecke, and every friend and family member who shared their stories with me so I could write this anthology. Special thanks to the members who patiently permitted me to interview them and harass them incessantly with endless inquiries: John and Josie Lorbiecke, Emmie Lianna Lorbiecke, Tracy John Babac, Hank Sisneros, Michaela Robertson, Samantha Robertson, and Stephanie Roberson, Julie Aguayo, Teresa and Marcos Bravo, Teri Soto, Mary Ann Martinuk, Mary Aguayo, Tausha, Kathy Aguayo, Ernest Aguayo, Dimitris Rentzios, Alethea Rentzios, Merie Bright, Oscar Villareal, Mario Villareal, Lori Aguayo, Vance Revell, Judy Burman, Sue Mosbrucker, Alice Cullinan, Harriet Ames, and everyone else who is mentioned or played a part in my journey.

Table of Contents

Dedication	i
Acknowledgment	ii
Prelude: Whispers Across Generations	p 11
Chapter 1: Eternal Love Among Revolution:	p 14
Chapter 2: Gabriel and La Lechuza	p 23
Chapter 3: Mi Amor	p 25
Chapter 4: Mary Ann and Mother Superior	p 27
Chapter 5: Café con Leche	p 31
Chapter 6: Haunting of the Murphy House	p 36
Chapter 7: Whispers of the Night	p 60
Chapter 8: Cursed Fortune of Blackfoot	p 66
Chapter 9: Night Terror	p 69
Chapter 10: Terrifying Tale	p 71
Chapter 11: Creature in Corvallis	p 74
Chapter 12: Fiery Eyes	p 76
Chapter 13: Séance in the Cemetery	p 78
Chapter 14: Haunting on Harry Street	p 83
Chapter 15: Grandpa's Last Smile:	p 86
Chapter 16: Final Farewell	p 88
Chapter 17: Ollie's Home	p 91
Chapter 18: Not Pep	p 93
Chapter 19: Creole Cat	p 96
Chapter 20: UFO & Ghost Parson Ranch	p 98
Chapter 21: Lady of Light	p 118

Table of Contents

Chapter 22: Echoes of Cosmic Reminiscence — p 121
Chapter 23: Man Bygone — p 133
Chapter 24: Phantom of the Silage — p 135
Chapter 25: Abandoned House Thriller — p 137
Chapter 26: Starry Night — p 139
Chapter 27: Dawn Departure — p 141
Chapter 28: Super Charger B Luminous Orb — p 144
Chapter 29: Cherub's Flight — p 147
Chapter 30: Bounty Hunter Immortal — p 150
Chapter 31: Lechuza in Victoria — p 154
Chapter 32: The Joke's on You — p 156
Chapter 33: Lost Soul of Nahum — p 157
Chapter 34: Saved by the Boy — p 168
Chapter 35: Phantom of the Tribal Monastery — p 171
Chapter 36: Numen of the Night — p 174
Chapter 37: Phantom that Followed — p 182
Chapter 38: Journey Beyond — p 188
Chapter 39: Heart of Darkness — p 192
Chapter 40: Peeping Poltergeist — p 195
Chapter 41: Love Beyond the Veil — p 198
Chapter 42: Shade of The Shining — p 201
Chapter 43: Shadows — p 213
Chapter 44: Holiday Spirit — p 215
Chapter 45: Ghostly Watcher — p 218
Chapter 46: Roswell Parallel Universe — p 221
Chapter 47: Beelzebub — p 238
Chapter 48: Endless Night — p 2409

Table of Contents

Chapter 49: Astral Projection University	p 243
Chapter 50: Satan in the Fire	p 249
Chapter 51: Doppelganger of Quezon City	p 253
Chapter 52: Light Over Alien Country	p 256
Chapter 53: Haunted Lee House Black Forest	p 259
Chapter 54: Nightmare Rolling Hills Asylum	p 265
Chapter 55: Wicked Wendy	p 269
Chapter 56: Nightmare in Aurora	p 276
Chapter 57: Ufonautic Feline Watchers	p 279
Chapter 58: Bigfoot of Painted Rocks Lake	p 282
Chapter 59: Vanishing Car in Casper	p 286
Chapter 60: Catching Rainbows	p 288
Chapter 61: Let the Devil Take Me Tonight	p 291
Chapter 62: Ouija	p 297
Chapter 63: Guardian Angel on Ice	p 303
Chapter 64: Raven Child	p 307
Chapter 65: Tuxedoed Intruder	p 309
Chapter 66: Guardian of the Shadows	p 310
Chapter 67: Maria Dubois	p 315
Chapter 68: Eric Lingered	p 317
Chapter 69: Junior Boy	p 320
Chapter 70: Carolina Snow	p 322
Chapter 71: Shotgun Shadow	p 325
Chapter 72: Zariah's Angel	p 326
Chapter 73: Tank	p 327
Chapter 74: Footfalls	p 328
Chapter 75:Payton Eternal	p 332
Chapter 76: Night Visitor	p 336

Table of Contents

Chapter 77: Nocturnal Demon	p 338
Chapter 78: Incubus of Utah	p 340
Chapter 79: Lifesaving Elixir	p 343
Chapter 80: Calling Collect	p 347
Chapter 81: Telekinesis Kid	p 350
Chapter 82: Haunted Hunting Lodge	p 354
Chapter 83: Hunting ET	p 360
Chapter 84: The Brave Little Saucer	p 366
Chapter 85: Lead Caskets	p 369
Chapter 86: Grays	p 371
Chapter 87: Supersonic Orbs	p 374
Chapter 88: Anton Part Deux	p 377
Chapter 89: Time Loop	p 381
Chapter 90: Phantom of the Wigwam	p 387
Chapter 91: Fanboy Everlasting	p 396
Chapter 92: Conclusion	p 397
Author Biography	p 402
Epigraph	p 404

ACKNOWLEDGMENTS

With profound gratitude, I find myself compelled to convey my deepest appreciation to my family, whose unwavering support has been the fuel behind my journey as a writer. To my beloved John Daniel, you are the very embodiment of love in my life, my eternal companion, my closest confidant, and my unwavering advocate in all my endeavors. Your unwavering belief in me has fortified my spirit and given me the courage to chase my dreams relentlessly.

To Anton Isaac, my appreciation has no bounds for your ceaseless efforts, profound wisdom, and daily encouragement. You feed me. You water me. You massage me. Without your tireless work and insightful guidance, the dreams I hold dear would remain distant and unattainable. Your unwavering dedication continues to fuel my passion, and I am eternally in your debt.

Emmie Lianna, my cherished soul, you have been my refuge on the most challenging of days, always a listening ear and supporter. Your unwavering love and pride in my accomplishments fill my heart with boundless joy. I cannot find the words to express how deeply I love you and how immensely proud I am of the remarkable person you are becoming.

Special thanks go out to the phenomenal cover artists, Dimitris Rentzios and Merie Bright. Your skill and creative dedication brought this book to life. I cannot express my gratitude enough.

To every family member and friend who has joined me on this magical journey I call my life, I hold each of you in a special place within my heart. I can never adequately convey my appreciation for your unwavering support, strength, and reason. You are the pillars of my strength, the voices of wisdom, and the steadfast supporters who have made my pursuit of these passions a reality. Without all of you, this anthology could have become a reality.

With heartfelt love and immense gratitude,

Marita Christine Lorbiecke

Φορτεανσ Υνϖειλεδ: Φαμιλψ ςαυλτ οφ Συπερνατυραλ ανδ Παρανορμαλ

Prelude

Ethereal Whispers Across Generations

The Aguayo family's storied history unfolds in the heart of Mexico, where vibrant indigenous and colonial cultures converged amid ancient mysteries. In the late 1800s, Gabriel and Carmen Aguayo, founders of this enigmatic lineage, embarked on a love story that defied the odds. Gabriel, a spirited freedom fighter, rescued an indigenous girl from violent raiders, forever intertwining their destinies and igniting a love that would endure political upheaval. Carmen's luminous starry eyes held secrets, and their romance flourished within the challenges of a turbulent world.

In this five-generation saga, their love story founding writes a legacy that transcends time and space, shaping the fates binding the family to the mysteries of the universe. Passion and curiosity guide them through the labyrinth of the unknown and toward the secrets that surpass our understanding.

In the quiet corners of our world, the extraordinary exists beyond everyday perception. Within this family lies a chronicle of the uncanny, a journey into the mysterious, awe-inspiring, unsettling, and unbelievably true tales. Explore the ultimate anthology—a collection of anecdotes defying explanation. They danced with apparitions, wrestled with demons, and communed with angels.

These tales are more than paranormal encounters; they are a testament to the human spirit, a quest for understanding, and a relentless pursuit of truth. This family has sought knowledge beyond mortal comprehension, glimpsing the afterlife, touching reincarnation's edges, and venturing into the realms of divine esoteric wisdom, challenging humankind's boundaries.

Gazing at the night sky, they were enraptured by unexplained lights and denizens of unidentified flying objects. Their experiences stretch our understanding of the cosmos and our place, inviting contemplation of otherworldly intelligence and visitors from far-flung galaxies.

Readers journey through time and space, traversing the blurry boundary between the known and unknown, encountering entities from beyond, witnessing spectral apparitions, and pondering existence. These tales are not simply curiosities but windows into a world beyond our understanding—a world where obscurities are as enduring as the human spirit. Step into the great mystery, for here begins a saga of the unexplained, the mystical, and the otherworldly, where fact and folklore intertwine, and reality's boundaries become shambolic. Welcome to the journey—the legacy of one family's fortean encounters.

Eternal Love Among Revolution: The Odyssey of Gabriel & Carmen

    The patriarch of the Aguayo family, Gabriel Aguayo, was born July 14, 1879, in Mexico City. As he flourished and became a member of the elite and wealthy, he grew disgruntled with the oppressive rule of the Porfirio Díaz regime, which brought untold suffering to the people through exploitation and inequality.

Choosing to take a stand, he relinquished his life of privilege and joined the revolution of freedom fighters. Doroteo Arango, best known by the public as Pancho Villa, was their leader, with righteous fury and a burning desire for social justice. The suffering of his compatriots stoked his anger, the blood-soaked soil of his homeland, and the ruthless grip of foreign interests. His rage crystallized into a relentless determination to overthrow the corrupt forces that plagued Mexico, making him a fiercely enduring symbol of rebellion, driven to madness by the disparities. There were times when the band, while questing, raided the native villages of the indigenous, such as Tarahumara-Rarámuri, Yaqui, Mayo, and other indigenous groups in the northern state of Chihuahua. These groups were often directly impacted by the revolutionary turmoil in the region.

While marauding, Gabriel saw a beautiful tribal girl. When he noticed other militia members eyeing her, he took her for himself and protected her. He locked eyes on her. She turned to run. One of his comrades decided to beat him to the prize. She ran as the two men raced toward her, shrieking long hair flying. As the other raiders killed and pillaged them, Gabriel was overcome by his need to rescue her. While villagers were maimed and robbed, he swooped down, snatched her, and swung her onto the front of his horse. He wrapped one arm around her, sheltering her from the mayhem.

Eyes closed, terrified and lost, Carmen held on tight, with nowhere to go now that her home had been destroyed but with him. Although a wild, gruff man, he cared for her tenderly. Time passed, seasons changed, and the girl grew into a vibrant woman. Although young Carmen had witnessed Gabriel commit unspeakable acts, she had also seen him display courage and that his heart was one of justice. She noticed the love and tenderness he held for her like no other.

In time, she fell in love with her protector. Their relationship evolved from one of guardianship to a tempestuous romance, at times firey and at other times volatile. Though unusually petite, Carmen was an ardent, determined, and powerful woman. 1920 the revolution was over, and the militia men settled down.

On July 20, 1923, Pancho Villa was ambushed and assassinated in Parral, Chihuahua, Mexico. Times for citizens were not always harmonious. Gabriel, a hardworking family man during the week, was also an ardent man who enjoyed socializing on the weekends. Carmen did not begrudge him drinking and dancing as long as he remained faithful and provided well for her.

One night, feeling he had stayed out too late, she donned her shoes and shawl, searching for him. Carmen found him. Much to her dismay, he was deep in conversation with an alluring woman perched lustily on his knee.

His wife erupted into a tempest of fury. Once calm pools, her eyes were raging fires, burning with an intense searing steel. Her chest heaved with every breath. Her hands, trembling with indignation, clenched into fists, ready to shatter the world. Her voice, a thunderclap of wrath, echoed through the room, each word a torrent of resentment. The air crackled with raging energy, a storm unleashing ferocity. Her face, a mask of anger, bore witness to a tempestuous sea of raging emotions.

In her madness, she unsheathed the blade strapped to her thigh for protection and, without introduction or warning, sunk it deep into the woman's throat. As Carmen returned to her senses, she found herself in a pool, her victim's blood, her target gasping for breath as she held the spurts erupting from her neck.

Carmen's rage transformed into fear, and she looked at her husband. She was a sight to behold, a woman unshackled from all constraints, a whirlwind that brooked no resistance now meek and doe-eyed in the middle of a blood bath. Gabriel stood up and whirled around. Having seen crimes of passion committed in his life, he swallowed his shock and swept his repentant wife up in his arms. They fled. She was sheltered in his arms as onlookers crowded around the nameless woman. So fast it happened the other partygoers were left confused. The woman sputtered and choked as the couple ran out into the night. They made a plan to flee the country.

Rushing home, they spoke to Gabriel's friends. Not disclosing their predicament, they claimed they should move on since the revolution was over, and their leader was gone. They made a plan to cross the border into Texas. Traveling hastily, Gabriel, Carmen, and six other couples traveled by wagon, camping together at night and preparing campsite meals. As they trekked, Gabriel became offended by the women's attitudes toward Carmen. They considered her lower in rank than them since she was indigenous. He argued with them, saying he wouldn't accept them if they didn't respect her. When the travelers reached Victoria, Texas, Gabriel and Carmen chose to break away while the rest of the group traveled 80 miles further north to San Antonio, Texas.

They set down roots there. In time, their family grew from two to several, beginning with the birth of Antonia. Next came Marcos, followed by Juanita, Anita, Luisa, and finally baby Pedro. Each child became a chapter in their family's remarkable journey through time. After several years of isolation, in the mid-'50s, the old friends reached back out to Gabriel, and he forgave them conditionally. When traveling solo in the area of San Antonio vending precious metals, he would accept their invitation for coffee and a visit but never disrespected Carmen by reciprocating the invitation to Victoria, and they were still not welcome within his home. The couple lived married and deeply in love until Gabriels passed on March 23, 1970, at 90, and Carmen nine years later, on January 2, 1979.

La Lechuza

In Mexican folklore, the Lechuza is a supernatural creature associated with myths and superstitions. She is described as a sorceress who transforms from a beautiful woman into a large nocturnal bird, allowing her to move unnoticed to carry out her malevolent activities. She may perch on rooftops of individuals' homes she holds grudges against, often portrayed as a vengeful spirit of dark magic seeking retribution, targeting those who have wronged her or others. She is blamed for misfortunes and tragedies and is known for her bloodcurdling screams that foretell death or disaster. Legend claims she abducts individuals who have crossed her or committed wrongdoings.

La Lechuza's presence is seen as an omen of impending doom. People may engage in various rituals or protective measures to ward off the Lechuza and protect themselves from her evil, like reciting prayers, using charms, placing salt in a doorway, or avoiding certain behaviors or places associated with the creature. This figure and the telling of her tales add to the rich tapestry of Latin American folklore and cultural beliefs.

Gabriel and La Lechuza

The moon hung low in the cloudless sky, casting shadows across the old, weather-beaten hacienda. A sense of foreboding filled the air as Gabriel, now a father, ventured outside, drawn by an unsettling presence. Glancing around, senses on high alert, he saw no one. The wind whispered secrets, rustling the leaves of the ancient oak trees that stood sentinel in the courtyard. Heading back inside, a shadow swooped down. It was a monstrous owl, eyes of glowing embers. In a flash, the creature's talons closed around Gabriel's shoulders, its vise grip tightening.

"Lechuza!" Carmen's voice rang out from the window. Her delicate frame emerged from the darkness, fury burning. In trembling hands, she clutched a bullwhip, a family heirloom. She knew what she had to do.

The tar black feathers of the lechuza shone. She hissed and spat curses at Carmen, her words dripping with menace as Carmen swung and cracked the whip. Heart racing, Carmen raised her voice in prayer, the words tumbling from her lips like a protective barrier against the darkness.
The ancient incantations worked their magic, and the lechuza's grip began to weaken. The beast released an earth-shattering screech, unclutching Gabriel from her grasp. The man stumbled back, gasping for breath, wide-eyed with terror. Carmen, her voice unwavering, fixed the creature with a withering gaze.

"If you ever come back," she snarled, her voice laced with venom, "I'll kill you." The lechuza, defeated and fearful of Carmen, unfurled her wings, flapping off into the night, disappearing into the obscurity from whence it came. The hacienda fell silent again, the moonlight bathing the courtyard in an otherworldly glow. Carmen lowered the whip, her trembling hands now steady. She knew the lechuza would think twice before venturing near her family again. The power of her love and determination was more robust than any creature of the night.

Mi Amor

Decades later, when the two had grown into contented grandparents, Mary Ann, the child of their daughter Dolores, went to the hacienda to spend time in the summer with her grandparents. They seemed to her to be sedate, gentle folks from a distant land. She sat long, cherished hours with her Guelito, listening to his stories. He would point out the letters in the paper, and when she recited them back, he would call her clever and reward her with a kiss on the cheek. Mary Ann woke up early to listen to the birds. Her grandparents would rise, sit quietly in each other's presence, and have coffee together.

After a bit, Guelito would wander into the market and run a few errands. He would say hello to the grocer and ask the butcher about next week's sales. He would spend a nickel on a newspaper and stop by the bakery to buy one sweet bread, a Mexican pastry. He and his Carmenita would sit in the garden when he wandered back. He would break the treat in two, always offering her the larger half. He would kiss her hands, tell her she was his beautiful love, and read her the paper as they shared the delicate, flaky pastry.

Mary Ann grew up lovely and showed the family how astute she was. She was very successful in college and became comfortably wealthy. When she achieved a new benchmark in life, she often remembered her grandfather's tender words of encouragement. She remembered his gentle heart and always chose to love and care well for those she loved best. From her grandmother, she inherited her ferocity and strong faith, knowing that nothing could stand against her if she were unflinchingly brave and ever faithful. This she does very well to this day. She had two sons, one of whom you will meet in a future chapter.

Μαριτα Χηριστινε Λορβιεχκε

Mary Ann & Mother Superior

When only twelve, Mary Ann was traveling to her grandparents' house. Disembarking the train, she hailed a cabby to travel the remaining distance. A car stopped, and she hopped in, the upcoming reunion on her mind. She was smiling as the car pulled out. He wasted no time asking uncomfortably personal questions. Mary Ann clammed up, noticing the driver, moving his mirror and staring, his bulging eyes wandering all over her. He complimented her on her glossy black hair and pretty dress. Mary Ann tugged her sweater closed, crossing her arms across her chest. He persisted, telling her he really liked her smile, raking dirty fingers through greasy hair. She grimaced, eyes narrowed into slits, staring blankly out the window, making sure not to encourage his crude advances as she roiled with rage.

She thought he was a nasty toad and wondered if he had hurt any passengers. He brazenly asked if she had a boyfriend.

She responded with a barbed, "No." staring him down less than demurely. Wounded, he looked away, eyes on the road once again. This predator was accustomed to less thorny victims. As the car bumped along the rough roads, she caught his gaze raking over her again.

"You know, there's a turn-off up here where love birds go to be alone," he intimated. "It's pretty up there." When she didn't reply, he felt emboldened. "I could show you. It's right up here," he pointed, watching her reflection. You're a schoolgirl. I can tell," He mused. Looking back at him, she could see that his idea of a schoolgirl and hers were two different animals. "Do you go to school? He pestered. An idea struck her.

"I do. Well, I don't just go. I live there, at the nunnery. Santa María de las Ángeles Nunnery," she fibbed cunningly. He blanched. She smiled widely and looked at him with false longing. "I feel truly blessed to have found my calling. The opportunity to take my vow of chastity brings me joy. I look forward to dedicating myself entirely to God's service." She blinked boldly, watching him become squeamish.

"You're a nun?" he asked, his lechery shriveling tangibly from the driver's seat.

"Well, not fully, but soon. The Mother Superior has already chosen a date, this Easter. It's nearly here." His face went from white to green in pallor. "Thank you for getting me safely to my grandparents', Mister. It's right up there." She now grinned genuinely, knowing she had outwitted this ape. She rolled the window down and waved excitedly to her grandfather.

"Guelito! Guelito!" she called, encouraging him to approach the car to avoid any last-minute sweet talk. Hardly waiting for the vehicle to stop, she jumped out and ran into her grandfather's arms, tears welling.

"Mija?" Her grandfather hugged her in surprise. "Are you okay?"

"I'm just happy. I missed you," she whimpered, wiping her eyes. The nervous butterflies flew from her stomach as her grandmother came out, ushering her inside to a hot, comforting meal. She had considered that if there were a falsehood God would approve of, it was one to preserve a girl's innocence from a deviant.

She thought back to some of the stories she'd heard where her grandmother stood her ground or other stories where she'd used her wit to overcome and laughed out loud, thankful to be safe with the protection of the loving family.

Café con Leche

By New Year's Day of 1979, Carmen Herrera Aguayo, born July 16, 1886, had amassed a wealth of experiences and memories throughout her long, colorful life. Her family affectionately called her Guelita, the cherished mother, grandmother, and great-grandmother. At the age of 93, she had outlived her beloved Gabriel. She faced a daunting battle with a brain tumor that had left her bedridden, living out her final days in a sterile hospital room.

Amidst beeping machines and cold surroundings, her female relatives gathered, taking turns sitting near, providing comfort and patient company during the last precious days. The hospital became a temporary refuge, where they all shared in Guelita's final journey.

One night, Terri Soto, one of Guelita's many beloved granddaughters, sat vigil beside her. The dimly lit room held its breath as the clock ticked towards 10 pm. Guelita, with a frail yet determined voice, expressed a simple desire: café con leche, a cup of coffee with heavy cream.

Happy to meet her grandmother's request, Terri swiftly made her way to the hospital cafeteria, the distant murmur of nurses and the faint scent of antiseptic in the air. Two steaming cups of coffee were carefully procured, one for Guelita and one for herself, with just the right amount of cream and sugar to suit her grandmother's taste.

Upon her return, Terri gently handed the cup to Guelita, who held it with trembling hands, gratitude shining in her eyes. Then came an unexpected question that surprised Terri.

"Where's your Guelito's?"

Confusion clouded Terri's expression, not anticipating this request. Nevertheless, she saw no harm in humoring her grandmother's wish. She was beginning to lose touch with reality as she declined. With a heartfelt apology, Terri set her cup of coffee at her seat across the room and promptly returned to the cafeteria, determined to fulfill Guelita's heart's desire.

 The hospital hallway felt forsaken in the late hour, the overhead lights casting a pallid glow on the linoleum floor. Terri returned with a third cup of coffee, a silent promise to ensure her grandmother's comfort. However, when Terri reentered the room, a cold chill enveloped her. She saw the cup of coffee she had set aside for herself was nearly empty with no explanation, as her grandmother could not leave the bed without assistance. A chill prickled Terri as she grasped for understanding.

 Guelita, now sipping contentedly from her coffee, wore a knowing smile. Your Guelito thanks you, she smirked sweetly. It was as if she had been given a final, cherished gift—a simple coffee date with her long-lost love. Terri adjusted the quilt covering her grandmother's legs and sat down.

As the night wore on, Terri remained wide awake, her mind filled with wonder and curiosity about the mystery. She suspected that Guelita's passing was imminent. Terri was happy that, at that moment, Carmen had received her small wish, and when the veil was lifted, and she shared a moment with her late husband, it seemed only a prelude to the eternity they were preparing to share. Guelita's journey ended the next morning, filled with the warmth of family and love. It was a peaceful transition, and her memory lived on in the hearts of those who gathered around her—a testament to the enduring bond between generations.

Haunting of the Murphy House

Our story continues with Pedro, Gabriel, and Carmen's son, born in 1937 in Victoria, TX. Pedro met and married Dolores Chavez. The couple had children: nine-year-old Terri, seven-year-old Mary Ann, five-year-old Josie, three-year-old Pete, two-year-old Ernie, and baby Julie. Pedro worked hard but was far from a rich man. Saving up to buy a home, the family rented what they could afford.

Summers end of 1962, he was delighted to find a beautiful, spacious home at an unusually affordable price. It was early fall, which is still warm in southern Texas. Larger and statelier than any place they had lived before, the children surveyed the home with glee. It was an extravagant five-bedroom house with a considerable parlor, a dining room with a long table, and a full kitchen with honey-golden hardwood floors. Attached was a massive porch wrapping around two sides with lush waxy magnolias adorning the house and porch. Across a sprawling lawn was a giant windmill, which delicately crawled purple, luscious grapes neighbored by stately trees. This was the first home the family lived in with indoor plumbing. Most occupants would add rugs or carpets, but Pedro was saving. The family lived frugally. Acquiring this home for his growing family felt like a dream come true.

Once the family was settled, Pedro was often away, working or visiting. Neighbors and cousins enjoyed commiserating about the strenuous work week. This left Dolores and the children at home alone much of the time. It wasn't long before his wife began complaining about frightening occurrences she believed were evil. He would dispel her concerns in the hopes of negating her fears. When it persisted, and Dolores became upset, she would ask Terri to take charge so she could have a reprieve and visit with her cousins a few doors down.

When their mother was inside, the children instinctively gave her a wide berth. Although sometimes loving and kind, she was highly irritable due to the instability of her mental health. She was extraordinarily spiritual and devout Christian but believed herself to be attacked by evil forces. She was sensitive and often perceived what others could not. Some children were also discerning, but none as strongly as Delores.

The children busied themselves outside while Dolores performed her domestic duties. It was only a few weeks before she began to describe frightening visions. Half the house was closed off, with furniture in storage belonging to the homeowners. Three of the bedrooms were locked. Of the two remaining rooms, one was for the couple and the other for the children.

One overcast morning, the children were playing inside while Dolores was visiting her cousins, Tia Nieces, and Cruz, who lived nearby when the kids heard a peculiar squeaking coming from a locked room. Josie stopped playing and walked to the door. Mary Ann put her ear up to the door.

"What is that?" Josie, a girl of petite stature like her grandmother Carmen, was just the right height to squint and peer through the large skeleton keyhole in the brass handle. Her right eye closed, her left eye searching the room.

Piles of furniture from the turn of the century were stacked high. Wardrobes, trunks, an upholstered club chair, art deco paintings, an elegant Brentwood coffee table, a hand crank Victrola, piles of sparkling straight-cut dresses, and pointed shoes were all lined up, and in the middle of the room was a red maple rocking chair with delicately curving armrests and ornate spindles. The seat and backrest were upholstered in burgundy velvet. Josie giggled because she saw that chair begin to sway as she watched.

"Look!" she cooed. She was calling her older sisters.

"Let me see!" Mary Ann said, pushing Josie out of the way. Her mouth fell open, and she stood up, blinking.

"Let me." Terri insisted, shoving her sister. She blinked twice to ensure her eyes were working, then watched the chair rock steadily, the hair on the back of her neck raising.

We're going outside," Terri directed as she rounded up the children, pushing them, holding toddling Ernie's hand, and handing Julie to Mary Ann. The older girls shook their heads as Josie continued asking who was rocking the chair. Her sisters shushed her and told her to stop talking about it.

One chilly evening, Josie and Pete were in a bath. The children splashed and played as their mother soaped their hair and poured warm water. She was using a bowl that had been removed from the dishes. It was no longer in the kitchen because a metal cereal bowl had gotten a ding, leaving a viciously sharp edge. It was no longer safe for the children to eat out of, but it worked fine for dipping and pouring water. Dolores stepped out of the bathroom, momentarily calling Mary Ann to bring a towel.

A dark entity appeared, lifting the bowl out of the bath water. Josie watched, transfixed, as the water slowly poured out like a gentle waterfall. Violently, the bowl came down atop Josie's head, splitting her scalp with the jagged edge. Blood poured into the water. Josie shrieked. Dolores ran in and grabbed her daughter out of the water, thinking Pete had hit her. She wrapped Josie in a towel and ran down the street to her neighbor's house to beg a ride to the hospital. Terri rinsed Pete and took him out of the bathwater. She wrapped him up, hugging him close. Josie's head was patched up.

One rainy afternoon, the kids were playing indoors while their mother was out, and the girls' curiosity got the better of them. They couldn't resist the temptation to peek beneath the creaky door of one of the mysterious locked rooms. Peering under the narrow gap, hair rising as the room revealed secrets. Elusive murmurs and shadows flickered and swayed in a ghostly dance, accompanied by the faint strains of swing music. The atmosphere grew increasingly dreadful, and an unsettling chill settled into their bones. A shared, uneasy glance between them conveyed the unspoken consensus—time to end their clandestine exploration of the forbidden rooms. With sweaty palms, they retreated quietly, realizing that some mysteries were perhaps best left unsolved lest they delve too deep into the enigmatic nature of their home.

One moonlit night, Pedro returned home late, his footsteps echoing in the still of the dark. Having spent the evening in animated socialization, his laughter mingled with the night's chorus of crickets. As Pedro approached the house, an odd sight halted him. The children's blankets lay strewn across the yard, like forgotten memories scattered by spectral hands. Foreboding crept over him as he entered the dimly lit interior.

Inside, his little ones slumbered peacefully, blissfully unaware of the strangeness that had unfolded outside. Pedro's furrowed brow betrayed his concern as he gently roused them from dreams, seeking answers. With sleepy eyes half closed, the children insisted they'd fallen asleep beneath their bedding and no one had entered their bedroom.

Unease gripped Pedro, recovering his bewildered children, their reassurances failing to quell his disquiet. Like elusive shadows, his thoughts darted back to Dolores' unsettling tales about ghostly apparitions and strange happenings. Momentarily, he considered a troubling possibility. Shaking the notion from his mind, he opted to cast aside supernatural speculations and reassure himself that all was well. Yet, beneath his facade of certainty, a lingering doubt remained an unspoken question that crept through the subconscious of his mind.

A week later, Josie woke up hearing tittering, feeling someone poking her foot and pulling on the blankets. She shook Terri but realized her big sister was already awake, eyes squeezed shut. Terri wrapped her arms around the smaller girl and whispered for her not to open her eyes.

"Pretend to be asleep and say your Hail Marys in your mind," Her sister whispered. "Just keep doing that, and they'll go away." Scared stiff, Josie did as she was told. Eventually, she fell back asleep.

During the hushed hours of many other nights, as the children nestled beneath their cozy blankets in the comforting embrace of their bed, they found themselves transported to a time and place immemorial. A nostalgic echo of a bygone era, soft strains of ragtime music would waft through the still of their room, the melody haunting yet strangely inviting. It was as if the walls of their home harbored secrets, revelry from another time, a chorus of notes and songs.

The sounds of boisterous partygoers often woke the youths, their laughter, and animated chatter resonating through the house. They exchanged puzzled glances in the dim glow of moonlight. They knew their parents were asleep.

Yet, the ghostly festivities persisted. Joy from days past chose their home as its eternal haunt. In their bedroom, the kids would listen to spirited celebrations unfolding. Enigmatic nights left them with a lingering sense of wonder and a nagging curiosity about the untold stories their home held within timeworn walls. These stories became an integral part of their dreams.

On Easter Sunday, the older children had catechism and came home to a meager but festive lunch. Crosses hung above each door, demonstrating the deep faith of the family. Mary Ann, a devoted girl, would kneel as she passed through every doorway and perform the ritual Sign of the Cross. She was first tapping her forehead. This action symbolizes the Father, the source of all creation, moving her hand down and touching her chest. This represents the Son, Jesus Christ, believed to have sacrificed himself for humanity's salvation. Then she would extend to touch her left shoulder, signifying the Holy Ghost, and finally, her right shoulder while reciting God the Father, God the Son, and God the Holy Ghost. Mary Ann was not only proud of her faith, she held steadfast to it, especially in times of duress.

The children were fast asleep that night when a bright light shone through their window like a flood lamp. Terri and Mary Ann both sat up, covering their eyes. Looking out the window, they could see the silhouettes of three massive magnanimous crosses stretching from the moon, nearly touching the Earth.

They went outside to behold the miraculous sight but did not see anything from out front. They went back inside and were overwhelmed by the image shining brightly. They woke up the other children to share in the sight. Josie was dancing and humming her favorite hymnal. Pete said it looked like the Virgin Mary, but all the girls said it looked like a shining cross, Jesus' cross. They were certain. Mary Ann said it was one giant cross, but Josie saw three. Terri kept going back and forth from outside, perplexed by why they couldn't see the lights from outside. In and out, they ran repeatedly but could not see any light except through the window. Ernie smiled and pointed, prattling. All the children danced and played in the chilly moonlight.

Usually, Dolores woke at the drop of a hat. Upon waking, the children would have been scolded for being out of bed. Throughout their celebration, she slept soundly this night, leaving the children to revel in their bliss. They all felt blessed by an Easter miracle, like a heavenly hug sent by their loving, holy Father to put them at ease during this time of difficulty.

As days passed, Dolores grew an increasingly troubled woman. A victim of grisly abuse as a child, she had unresolved trauma that sometimes gnawed at her psyche, coloring her state of mind. More than ever, the woman clung to her faith, calling on the power of her Lord and Savior to aid her rescue.

One day, she was washing dishes and unleashed a guttural scream. When the girls ran to help her, she explained that a man was watching her outside the window. Too afraid to investigate herself and with Pedro working, she sent Mary Ann outside to check. Terri and Mary Ann went out hand-in-hand but saw no one lurking. They weren't sure which idea was scarier. Their mother was plagued by ghosts or human evildoers snooping around up to no good while their father was away.

When Pedro started his truck in the mornings, he would see the neighbor Lucia's husband go off to work. The men would occasionally nod or wave to one another. On the days when his vehicle was erratic, and he was postponed, Pedro observed a gentleman caller drive up, park his car boldly in the driveway, knock, and be invited into the home by the missus. After a time, he would leave, tucking in shirt tails while heading to his car.

One afternoon, Lucia's husband confronted Pedro, asking him if he had seen anyone frequenting his home while he was away. Pedro replied that what happened in another man's home was not his affair and that if a man was concerned, he should return home at an unexpected hour and see for himself.

The next day, Lucia kissed her husband goodbye. He headed to work as she waved him off. Once there, he took care of a few duties, returned home, and checked in. Much to his chagrin, he found his wife entertaining a guest. A heated argument ensued, and Lucia's life became difficult. She could no longer accept new gentleman callers or socialize with the neighbor ladies.

For some reason, she got the idea that Dolores was the person who revealed her secret, tipping off her husband. For this, she held a vengeful grudge against Dolores. Years later, when Pedro took his niece, Rosemary, to see a curandera, the witch doctor told him she had a message for him. She sat him down in her temple and prepared an altar on the table. As she spoke, she revealed obscure details of his life that no stranger could know. She boiled and poured him a cup of herbal tea in a powder blue porcelain mug. She guided him to drink the tea while she lit a triangle of candles. When empty, she pressed the saucer to the top and flipped it over. By candlelight, she read the tea leaves. As she read them, she explained the following.

She told Pedro that the adulteress Lucia and her cousin had sought revenge on his wife for a perceived betrayal. Lucia and her cousin held a séance to curse Dolores. The two women lit dark candles and recited incantations invoking hostile forces to bring harm to their neighbor. Under the blaze of a haunting ambiance of a hex ritual, red candles flickered and sputtered as the two drew occult symbols of pentagrams to create a protective barrier toward themselves and invoke dark forces outward. They made a blood offering to gain favor with evil spirits. They summoned wickedness to haunt the woman, driving Dolores to her doom.

Pedro was informed that although the curse affected his wife, sometimes causing her to madness, she survived due to her strong will and even stronger faith. Not only did she endure, but when Dolores rebuked the enmity with prayers and chants, the energy was directed back to the women. Lucia's cousin inexplicably lost her sight after attempting to utilize her second sight to evoke harm on an innocent. Lucia paid the price, with her life meeting an unexpected and tragic end when she was still young.

As the paranormal events culminated in the house, driving Dolores to insanity and hearing the children complain of mystical experiences, Pedro gave in and agreed to vacate the property. Even he couldn't deny the spooky feelings that oppressed him. With the decision made, Pedro made arrangements with the landlord and secured a new residence. He quickly packed all of the furniture. Except for the gas-burning stove, the heaviest, most cumbersome item to move, he had to wait for his cousin to help him carry it. He had placed the detachable metal grates from the burners into the sink while the men lifted and walked the stove out the front door and lifted it into the truck bed. His cousin climbed aboard the vehicle while Pedro returned to grab the burners.

Stepping indoors, he was perplexed to see the same home. However, instead of empty as it was a moment ago, it was entirely outfitted with plush cushioned seating, ornate, rich grain wooden furniture, and glamorous chandeliers that cast dim, sultry lighting, giving the impression of a clandestine atmosphere rather than a family home. There were paintings on the wall, and very faintly coming from the kitchen, the sound of music from the roaring '20s.

Shaking disbelieving, he walked into the kitchen to get the burners. When he reached into the sink basin, he noticed two glasses on the counter with fresh cocktails and condensation dripping. He swallowed hard, studying the martini with three olives in an elegant long-stemmed glass and the gin rickey over crushed ice in a highball rimmed with a fresh-cut lime. He pulled his hand back and turned around to see a flapper party in full swing as bobbed-haired women in glitzy fringed dresses with bright lipstick laughed loudly over the blaring music. Sharp-dressed men peacocked around them in gangster-style suits, oblivious to the man in their speakeasy. At this, Pedro abandoned his task and left the grates behind, running out of the house and slamming the door behind him. The stove loaded, he started the truck, and took off.

Body stiff as a board, he flew, sweat dripping into his eyes, and when he was about a quarter-mile down the drive, nearly back to the main road, he slammed on the brakes. As he slid to a stop, a dust cloud was rousted, obscuring his view.

With his shirt sleeve, he wiped his eyes and his forehead. As the dust cleared, he blinked slowly. His passenger, also spooked, although he had no idea why, stared petrified. Stomach-churning, Pedro pointed to the middle of the road where his headlights illuminated the four grates to the stove he had just left.

He left the house on Murphy Road that night, and no one in the family ever returned until Josie, now grown, her husband, John, and teenage son, JD, drove by it in 1986 and saw it had been burnt to the ground.

Through the years, as Dolores had these episodes, Pedro would lovingly take her to various curanderas for healing. He worked as a contractor all over Texas and took her with him. They would visit healers in Texas and Mexico. Curanderos have a long and rich history in Mexico and the American Southwest, where indigenous healing practices merged with European and African traditions to form a unique and diverse system of traditional medicine, with indigenous roots dating back thousands of years to pre-Columbian civilizations like the Aztecs and the Mayans.

Healers, *ticitl*, among the Aztecs, used herbal remedies, spiritual rituals, and energy manipulation to treat ailments. These practices were based on a holistic understanding of health, where an individual's physical, mental, and spiritual aspects are interconnected.

With the Spanish conquest of Mexico in the early 16th century, indigenous healing traditions encountered European influences, including Catholicism. Spanish friars and missionaries sought to convert indigenous people to Christianity, often incorporating Christian prayers and rituals into indigenous healing practices.

The terms "curandero" (male healer) and "curandera" (female healer) emerged during this period and became associated with those who practiced a blend of indigenous, European, and Christian healing techniques. The African slave trade also played a significant role in the development of curanderismo in the Americas. African healers brought their traditions, such as herbs, divination, and spiritual rituals, which influenced and intermingled with indigenous and European practices.

Over time, curanderos adapted and syncretized their healing traditions, creating a unique and complex system of folk medicine that incorporated elements of indigenous, European, and African cultures that utilize herbal remedies, spiritual cleansing, prayer, and rituals to address physical and spiritual ailments.

During the colonial period, the practice of curanderismo underwent scrutiny and suppression from colonial authorities and the church. It was often viewed as oppositional to the church and state. Despite this, curanderos continued to provide healthcare services to their communities underground. Curanderismo survived generations, especially in rural and indigenous communities. In the 20th and 21st centuries, there has been a resurgence of interest in traditional healing practices, including curanderismo. Many individuals seek out curanderos and curanderas for their expertise in herbal medicine, energy healing, and spiritual guidance, valued for their holistic healing and deep connection to cultural traditions.

Upon arrival, the curanderas often interview their clients, relying on their intuition or spirit guides to choose a treatment plan. They may do a variety of rituals depending on the ailment. They might perform a *limpia*, a cleansing removing negative energies or spiritual blockages from a person's energy field. It typically involves using herbs, flowers, eggs, or other symbolic objects. The curandera may pass these objects over the person's body or use them ritualistically to absorb and remove negativity.

Curanderas are often knowledgeable about the use of medicinal herbs and plants. They may prepare herbal remedies, teas, oils, or poultices to treat physical and spiritual ailments. These remedies are chosen based on the curandera's assessment of the person's condition. Curanderas often incorporate prayer and invocations into their healing practices. Depending on the curandera's background and beliefs, these prayers may be of Catholic, indigenous, or syncretic origin.

They may invoke spiritual entities or saints for guidance and protection. Some curanderas perform spiritual cleansing ceremonies that involve using sacred smoke, such as copal or sage, to purify a person's energy or living space. This is often accompanied by prayers and specific rituals.

Curanderas may use their hands to assess and manipulate a person's energy field. They may employ techniques like *pases* to channel healing energy or remove blockages. Some curanderas are skilled in divination methods, such as reading tarot cards, using pendulums, or practicing scrying, to gain insights into a person's situation and provide guidance. Curanderas may offer blessings and protection rituals to safeguard individuals or their homes from negative influences or spiritual harm. These rituals may involve holy water, crosses, or other protective symbols. Curanderas often interpret dreams as a means of understanding a person's spiritual and emotional state. They may provide guidance based on dream symbolism. The lighting of specific colored candles and inscribing symbols or names are standard practices in curanderismo. This is often done as part of a ritual to address a particular issue or intention.

Armed with this knowledge and more, Pedro took his beloved to the San Juan Pilgrimage after a particularly tumultuous time, known as the "Peregrinación de San Juan," held annually on June 24th and 25th to honor San Juan Bautista, Saint John the Baptist. It is one of Mexico's most important religious celebrations, attracting pilgrims nationwide, and the religious procession and pilgrimage are held in San Juan de los Lagos, Jalisco, Mexico. This pilgrimage is a profoundly religious, spiritual, communal, and cultural event seen as an opportunity for penance, purification, and divine intervention.

While it is not customary for participants to crawl the entire way on their knees, it is a specific act of devotion involving walking on one's knees. Delores chose to do so, clutching her medallion in hopes of healing from Christ. When home, it took weeks to heal from bruising and abrasions, and her joints never fully recovered. This was a powerful expression of faith and cultural tradition. The family believed it improved her condition for a time.

Refuge of the Fig

The Aguayo family settled into their new life in the quiet aftermath of their move from the Murphy house. The close-knit group moved into a charming little place, nestled beneath the branches of a majestic fig tree, on East Harry Street in Victoria, Texas. Pedro, Dolores, and their six children embarked on this chapter of their journey—Terri, Mary Ann, Josie, Pete, Ernie, and baby Julie.

A dilapidated building stood on the family's modest property, a feeble reminder of past neglect. Pedro had often talked about tearing it down, a project forever postponed by the demands of daily life. Terri, however, took matters into her own hands. With youthful determination, she climbed the nearby trellis and pushed against the ramshackle structure with her feet until it gave way. Though surprised, Pedro, far from angry, collected the fallen nails and stacked the lumber, ready to repurpose it.

But the tranquility of their new home concealed a shadow that would occasionally fall upon them. Dolores was not always herself. Inexplicable episodes of agitation would seize her, leading her into heated arguments with hidden forces. One fateful morning, her distress reached a crescendo as she fixated on an eerie, haunting tune that seemed to have trapped her soul. Terrified but composed, Terri, wise beyond her years, approached her mother gently, suggesting she lay down and rest. Dolores seemed to go into catalepsy and began to sing a sinister cradlesong. Terri watched her mother curiously. Dolores confessed.

Pulling out the largest kitchen knife, she spoke to Terri with an unsettling conviction, "I think it's time for me to leave this world and fly home today." With a heavy and relentless heart, Terri assured her mother that she could watch the children and prepare lunch while Dolores rested.

"No," her mother replied, "I think all you kids need to go home with me. We'll fly away together."

Dolores's hysteria materialized as she went from a nearly catatonic state to one of explosive energy in pursuit of Mary Ann. Desperate, her daughter ran for her life. Terri swiftly gathered her other siblings, except for Julie, cribbed in her parent's room. Trembling, Terri ushered her younger brothers and sisters out the back door, quiet as a cat. She hoisted them up into the sanctuary of the fig tree, where Mary Ann, who had crawled under the table and out of the washroom window, was already hiding.

Returning inside, Terri snuck into her mother's room, covered Julie's mouth, and skillfully navigated the treacherous terrain of her home, her senses sharp. With the baby in her arms, she ran outside and reached the tree, climbing up to join the others. They remained hidden within the branches throughout the harrowing afternoon, anxiously awaiting their father's return.

From that day forward, Pedro would wake Terri at 4:30 each morning, when he departed for work, to keep vigil over the rest of his children. Dolores's nocturnal wanderings became a frightening event in the household. Sometimes, she meandered peacefully, methodically planning her duties.

Other times, she whispered incoherently, lost in the depths of her mind, rocking back and forth in her chair. Clinging to her sibling, she could gauge her mother's location by her troubled whispering and the rhythmic squeaking of the chair. If the creaking ceased, an icy panic would grip Terri, her senses sharpening to the slightest sound. Listening, with bated breath, unable to swallow until the familiar creaking of the chair resumed.

When Dolores's rocking ceased, and her humming morphed into an eerie lullaby, Terri would send her siblings away with Mary Ann and stealthily navigate the house, locate Julie, slip through a window, and disappear into the shadows. There, they would remain, hidden away, until their father returned.

There were times when Terri could hear someone outside moving that lumber from the torn-down shed from one side of the yard to the other. From east to west, someone would drag heavy boards for hours. Their bedroom window did not face the backyard. Electing not to leave the others to investigate, Terri never knew who it was or why they were doing so.

In the heart of this familial struggle, Terri emerged as the unwavering shield for her siblings, a sentinel against the darkness that sometimes clouded their lives. In the depths of their journey, they found strength and resilience in each other's protective embrace. As they weathered the storms of Dolores's unpredictable episodes, the fig tree became their sanctuary, its branches sheltering them from the unknown. With Terri the protector and fearless Mary Ann, the children's courage and determination held their fragile world together until their father provided the safety for which they yearned. In the face of adversity, the family learned that love and unity were their greatest defenses and that there was always hope, even in the darkest moments.

Whispers of the Night

In 1954, Pedro wandered the dusty streets of Victoria, Texas, during the dreamy heat of a summer evening. The yearning for adventure had led him down a winding path, and as he strolled past the dimly lit cemetery that hummed of forgotten souls, he noticed her—a vision of beauty beneath the moon's pale glow.

She stood there, her form swathed in an ethereal mist, her lengthy hair cascading like a midnight waterfall down her back. Her presence seemed otherworldly, captivating Pedro in an instant.

He approached her with a charming smile and an audacious heart, hoping to initiate a conversation that would transcend time. The mysterious woman remained silent. Her gaze fixed on the horizon as if lost in the secrets of the night. Undeterred, Pedro took a daring step, draping his arm gently around her shoulders, hoping to bridge the gap between the living and the enigmatic beauty before him.

Just then, the piercing headlights of a passing Chevrolet Bel Air illuminated her face, and Pedro's heart froze. The enchantress was no woman. She was a skeleton, her eye sockets hollow voids, her smile a macabre grin that spoke of death's embrace. Terror coursed through his veins; his breath caught in his throat as the ghastly truth revealed itself.

With a scream that shattered the silence of the night, Pedro recoiled, stumbling backward in a frantic bid to escape the unearthly specter. His heart raced, and his mind reeled as he fled from the cemetery, leaving behind the haunting vision that would forever follow him through his dreams, a nocturnal encounter with the beautiful specter of death. A chilling reminder that even in the nostalgic embrace of a Texas summer night, the past could reach out to touch the living in the most bone-chilling of ways.

Μαριτα Χηριστινε Λορβιεχκε

Cursed Fortune of Blackfoot

In the quiet town of Blackfoot, Idaho, in an ordinary apartment on a sleepy street lived the daughter of Pedro and Dolores, Terri, her husband Shaddy Villareal, and their infant son, Oscar, lived, unaware of the spectral presence that would soon disrupt their lives. A streetlight outside cast a ghastly glow through the window, turning the wall into a canvas of shadows and whispers.

One night, Terri lay in bed between baby Oscar and Shaddy. Rousing from her slumber, she saw a ghostly figure appear by the wall near the window. Heart fear-clenched, she watched it pass the mirror. The apparition of a woman draped in a long dress and a veil floated soundlessly through the room and into the kitchen.

Terrified in the dim reflection of the mirror, Terri watched as the poltergeist moved about the kitchen. Dishes began to slam against each other with a violent force that shattered the stillness of the night, waking Shaddy. With trembling hands, they flipped on the lights and cautiously opened the door to the kitchen, their breaths held in anticipation. To their bewilderment, nothing was amiss. Not a dish out of place, no sign of the intrusion.

Years later, another couple named Ray and Ramona moved into the same apartment, and they, too, found themselves haunted. The building's unsettling history would only reveal its sinister secrets when demolished. Hidden within the walls, they uncovered a stash of money that hinted at nefarious dealings and foul play from the past.

It became clear that the spirits lingering within those walls were unwilling to part with their hidden fortune, their restless souls tethered to the building by the greed that had consumed them in life. The haunting legacy of the apartment served as a chilling reminder that some secrets are so potent they linger long after death, and the pursuit of ill-gotten wealth can bind souls to this world in ways that defy both reason and the grave.

Night Terror

It was a moonless night when Terri lay in bed, heavily pregnant with her second son, Mario. The family was nestled in their humble home, sleeping comfortably. Oscar's crib stood by the wall. Terri snored gently beside her husband, Shaddy, who had fallen into a deep, alcohol-induced slumber. The world outside was wrapped in a profound silence, broken only by the faint rustle of leaves in the breeze. All seemed calm until a sudden disturbance shattered the tranquility. Terri was startled awake as Shaddy's elbow jabbed into her side. Confused and disoriented, she tried to shake him awake, but his eyes remained tightly shut.

Shaddy was disturbed by something more sinister than a dream. He shot up in bed, terror etched across his face, and his voice quivered as he whispered to Terri,

"Turn on the light! Do you see it?" The room remained shrouded in darkness as Shaddy's frantic cries filled the air. "It's in the closet!" Terri fumbled to switch on the bedside lamp, her heart pounding. She peered into the closet, spooked, but saw nothing out of the ordinary.

Shaddy, on the other hand, was trembling uncontrollably, his eyes fixated on the closet door. He rambled on, describing the dark figure of a native man with piercing red eyes, a graphically gruesome apparition that had terrorized him in the dead of night and hours dragged on, with Shaddy refusing to close his eyes, his fear casting a long shadow over their once peaceful abode. Terri, heavily pregnant, grew fatigued and yearned for rest, but her husband's paralyzing fear held them both hostage until the first rays of dawn broke.

As the sun's gentle light streamed into the room, Shaddy finally allowed Terri to turn off the lamp. He collapsed, exhausted and shaken, a silent witness to a horrifying encounter that defied explanation. The memory of that dreadful night would haunt their family, a constant reminder that, even in the security of one's home, terrors lurk in the shadows, waiting for the chance to seize upon innocent souls.

Terrifying Tale

In the heat of a sweltering summer, young Oscar, Terri's son, was in an unexpected predicament. He was visiting his grandparent's ranch, a place of dusty trails and scorching sun, far removed from the city's noise. While his grandparents were busy with chores, Oscar, ever curious, explored the property's nooks and crannies.

A misstep sent him tumbling into the gaping hole as he wandered near an old, disused septic tank. Panic surged through him, flailing and clawing as he realized he could not climb out. Trapped. Desperation gripped him. He screamed for help. The vast emptiness swallowed his cries.

Terror intensified when he felt a presence in the dim, dusty depths. Turning his head, choked with dread, he saw her, La Lechuza, the dreaded owl witch of Mexican folklore. There she perched, black feathers flashing, diabolical eyes gleaming with a venom that pierced Oscar's soul.

"Help! Help!" he shrieked, voice quivering. Outside, his grandparents heard his frantic cries and rushed to find him. With all their strength, they pulled him from the hole, relief palpable. Listening to his babbling wails, they scanned the surroundings but saw no sign of the dreaded lechuza. Oscar wept, body trembling with the memory of that harrowing encounter.

He recounted the chilling tale to his grandparents, who dismissed it as a child's overactive imagination, attributing it to the shock of his fall. Deep down, Oscar knew what he had seen—the ominous, unexplainable presence of La Lechuza. From that day forward, the memory of that encounter haunted his dreams and cast a shadow over his knowledge of what is real and what is imagined.

Creature in Corvallis

On the quiet confines of Bailey Lane in Corvallis, Montana, stood an old house, its timeworn walls steeped in history and stories untold. Joe, son of Alfredo and Julia Chavez, a young boy with a mop of unruly hair, had come to visit his grandparents, seeking solace in the familiar warmth of their home. The tranquility of the afternoon was shattered when, amid a peaceful slumber, Joe's grandfather's face contorted in agony. His grandma, ever vigilant, was the first to notice, her heart quickening.

She reached out to shake Alfredo awake, trembling in expectation of his reaction. Grandpa, caught in the throes of a nightmarish dream, fought back with a force that sent a shudder through her.

"Wake up!" she implored, her voice quivering with urgency. Finally, with a jolt, Grandpa awoke, his chest heaving as if he had been running from an evil force. In the dim light of the bedroom, he recounted the gripping nightmare—a massive, sinister bird, its ebony feathers like a shroud, had descended upon him in his sleep. Perched on his chest, it pressed the life out of him with a weight that defied reason. Its talons, sharp as daggers, slashed him without mercy.

Drenched in sweat, Grandma's trembling hands struggled to unbutton Alfredo's shirt, revealing a sight that would send chills through their collective souls. Angry red slashes and swollen, seeping battle scars marred the man's chest. Their ominous substantiation was undeniable. Fear clouded the room as the three exchanged wide-eyed glances, hearts heavy with the terror of what had just transpired. The house on Bailey Lane, once a haven of peace, now held secrets that would haunt their nights for years to come.

Fiery Eyes

In 1970, Joe, Son of Alfredo and Julia, and his wife Dorothy moved into an apartment that whispered secrets of the supernatural. Located in an old, innocuous building, it became clear that their new abode harbored peculiar, otherworldly secrets. As the sun dipped below the horizon, Joe and Dorothy lived out a routine existence: work, clean up, and have supper, often lit by the flickering glow of candles. There were occasions when the candles had their mind, mysteriously turning on and off without rhyme or reason. The room would come to life with dancing shadows, leaving the couple in perpetual unease.

One dreadful night, they lay in bed cocooned in their blankets, and they were jolted awake by a sight that defied logic. Two fiery red eyes, blazing unearthly, hovered in the darkness. Panic seized them, and Joe grabbed a nearby pillow, hurling it at the apparition with all the courage he could muster. To their horror, the pillow passed through the phantom as if it were made of smoke and mirrors.

Their terror intensified when they reached down to retrieve the pillow and found it hot to the touch, wisps of smoke curling from the singed fabric. Fear gnawed at their hearts, and they knew they could no longer stay in this spectral enclave. With frayed nerves, they packed their belongings and vacated the property, leaving behind the haunting presence that had permeated their lives.

Séance in the Cemetery

At midnight on a breezy summer night, Charo, Chip, Oscar, Mario, and their grandparents Alfredo and Julia gathered in the heart of the Texas countryside so Charo could receive a cleansing ritual. Among them was a wise mystic known for her powerful abilities. Chip was a curious boy with a penchant for the supernatural. Charo, his brother, was a bit of a skeptic. The group also included Oscar and Mario, two brothers known for their daring nature, and their beloved grandparents who had witnessed more than their fair share of life's mysteries.

Tonight, was earmarked for a ritual which had been passed down through generations. The moon cast animated shadows on the group huddled around Charo. The curandera held three candles: red, white, and black.
Charo heard her chant in an unknown tongue that danced with the wind. The air grew heavy with conviction. She prayed to the ancient spirits, calling upon their guidance and protection. The torches flickered, and the world blurred the ritual undertaken.

She beckoned to the boys, Oscar and Mario, both on the cusp of adolescence, to assist her. Trepidation in their eyes, they crossed over to the site of her alter.

The witch doctor warned them, "Before these candles burn out, you must complete the cleanse, or the consequences will be dire." They looked at each other, eyes brimming with fear.

"Don't stare into the flame," she warned. "Doing so can lead you down a path of money, but you will suffer along the way." Bashful and with sweaty palms, the brothers listened. As she directed, they sprinkled offerings of sacred herbs into the flames, watched as the smoke spiraled upward, and felt the weight of generations of curanderas and their knowledge impressing upon them.

As the red candle burned, the boys felt a rush of energy, being purified from within. With the white candle, they saw visions of a bright and hopeful future. But as the black candle's flame danced on its last wick, a shadowy figure appeared, a malevolent presence threatening them.
The healer chanted fiercely, drawing upon all her power. The brothers joined their voices with hers, their familial bond strengthening their resolve. The dark force recoiled, defeated and vanished into the ether.

Charo, Oscar, and Mario stood triumphant with the last candle extinguished. They had cleansed their family and land of an ancient curse of the lechuza plaguing their family, but they knew that the spirits would always be watching. They rejoined Grandma and Grandpa, whose ages and experiences serve as a testament to the enduring power of love, family, and the mystical traditions of Mexico. Once again, the curandera protected her kin from the darkness that sought to claim them.

Haunting on Harry Street

In the nostalgic backdrop of the 1960s, young Josie found herself drawn back to the old family home on Harry Street in Victoria, Texas. The old fig tree was now a towering guardian. The passing of her beloved Guelito, grandfather Gabriel Aguayo, had left an emptiness in her heart that only returning to the place filled with cherished memories could hope to mend. Little did she know, those memories would soon be tinged with an otherworldly presence. A chill prickled Josie as she entered the house. The house of long-lost recollections was congested heavily with energy. The flickering light of the hallway barely penetrated the thick shroud of darkness swathing the rooms. Cautiously, she walked through the house, footsteps echoing in the stillness.

Out of nowhere, she heard a haunting sound that halted her in her tracks. The unmistakable, agonizing drag of a leg across the wooden floor, a sound that seemed too real to be imagined.

"Guelito?" she called out, her voice quivering with fear and longing. There was no reply, only the relentless, ghostly sound of the dragging leg drawing nearer. Josie's heart pounded. Her breath quickened, beads of sweat forming on her brow. She clenched and unclenched her hands, whispering a prayer.

Her mind ran wild with thoughts of her dear Guelito, gone but not forgotten, and the inexplicable presence that seemed to linger in the darkness. In a daring moment, Josie mustered the courage to approach the source of the unsettling noise. The darkness thickened around her as she drew closer. She could feel a presence, a weight in the air. Shaking, she fumbled for the light switch.

With a click, the room flooded with light, revealing an empty, undisturbed space. No one was there, and the dragging sound had ceased. Josie stood alone in the room, her heart heavy with relief and sadness. As she continued her journey through the old house, she couldn't shake the feeling that Guelito's spirit lingered, perhaps to say one last goodbye, to remind her that love endures even in the darkest moments. The time in Josie's life was a time of change and upheaval. Still, in that timeless house on Harry Street, the bond between Josie and her grandfather transcended the boundaries of life and death, a comforting thought that lingered long after the echoes of that haunting leg drag had faded into memory.

Grandpa's Last Smile

In the heart of Corvallis, Montana, perched on Bailey Lane, stood Grandpa Alfred Chavez's home, a place filled with love, warmth, and childhood memories. For Josie, who was not much more than a toddler, this house held a special kind of magic and a hint of fearful wonder. The bedroom was a source of both comfort and trepidation for Josephine. She had always been too small to reach the string on the light fixture that would banish the darkness and illuminate the path to the bathroom. The fear of what lurked in the shadows often held her back. But her determination was as bright as the morning sun, and she devised a plan. Climbing onto the bed, she would crawl up the headboard, her tiny fingers reaching out, yearning to grasp the elusive cord vanquishing the dark.

After the passing of her beloved Grandpa Alfred, Josie returned to his home with a mix of nostalgia and sadness. The house felt different now like a part of its soul had departed with him. On one visit, she retraced her old routine, clambering to reach the light cord. But when she looked across the room, her heart nearly stopped. A figure stood there, a presence that defied logic. She was covered in goosebumps. Grandpa Alfred was sitting in his favorite chair, his warm smile reaching out to her from beyond the veil of the living. He wore the same clothes she had seen him buried in the day prior, a reassuring though startling sight. Blinking in disbelief, Josie watched as the apparition smiled at her, the bond between grandchild and grandparent transcending the boundaries of life and death.

With a blink, the room returned to emptiness, the chair vacant again. Shaken to her core, Josie clung to the bedspread, overwhelmed as she grappled with the profound encounter. Grandpa Alfred's final smile had bridged the gap between the worlds, leaving an indelible mark on her soul and a memory that would comfort her throughout her life.

Final Farewell

In 1988, in the quiet town of Park City, Montana, friends and family gathered to pay their respects at the wake of Jessie Chavez, son of Alfredo and Julia and beloved uncle to Mary Ann and Josie. Mary Ann and her husband, Tom Rentzios, had come to pick up her sister Josie, offering her a comforting presence during this somber occasion.

The threesome set out on the road to Park City, where the wake would be held. A heavy silence hung over the car, the reality of Jessie's passing casting a shadow over their thoughts.

Cloaked in sadness, Josie stared out the window contemplatively, her mind a whirlwind of memories. Upon their arrival, the mood was somber. Josie could feel the weight of Jessie's absence. She joined the mourners in paying her respects, exchanging stories of their shared times. But as the night grew darker, she sensed that Jessie wasn't long for this world.

Turning away from the crowd, Josie saw something that defied reason. There, leaning against a dresser, stood the unwavering image of Jessie Chavez himself, his apparition beaming at her with warm familiarity.

"You thought you were going to get away without seeing me. Didn't you," he quipped, his voice a spectral whisper. Alarm gripped Josie, and the lines between reality and the supernatural blurred. Not wanting the phantom to follow her home, she ignored the presence. Gradually, the apparition began to dissipate, fading away into the hereafter.

As the night wore on, Josie felt a sense of closure. The memory of Jessie's mischievous grin remained etched in her mind, a bittersweet reminder of her uncle, who, like so many others in her life, had passed beyond the veil but had returned one last time to bid farewell. The journey back to Hamilton was sad, but the fear had given way to a profound sense of acceptance, and the memory of Jessie's apparition would forever be a part of her journey through life.

Ollie's Home

In 1997, John and Josie Lorbiecke embarked on a journey back to their roots, returning to the tranquil embrace of Hamilton, Montana, in response to a final wish from Aloysius, Ollie, Lorbiecke, John's late father. Ollie's parting words to his son were clear: Move back home and build a house on the land I left you. Years later, when their only son JD had grown and ventured into the world, John and his wife decided to fulfill Ollie's dream.

As they built their new home, they camped in a cozy motorhome on the sprawling acreage Ollie had bequeathed. Evenings in Hamilton were a delight. The vast Montana landscape stretched before them. A tapestry of rugged beauty bathed in the golden hues of the setting sun. With the day's labor behind them, the couple retired, lounging in the front seat of their pickup, gazing out across the undulating terrain, savoring the serenity with a drink.

As the setting sun turned the landscape from gold to indigo, Josie, a seasoned observer of ghostly phenomena, felt a peculiar presence in the truck's back seat. Slowly, she turned around her senses on high alert. Sitting in the dim twilight was old Ollie, gazing out over his beloved land. His spectral presence carried a self-satisfied smirk, a testament to his joy at seeing his son and daughter-in-law fulfill his heartfelt wish.

"John," she told her husband, "Your father is here, and he's happy you're home." John chuckled, knowing that his wife could communicate with the other side. A man of very few words, he smiled, tapping out the beat of one of his father's old country songs on the steering wheel. He nodded, knowing his father's loving presence was contentedly at rest with them.

Not Pep

After the house had been constructed, the Lorbiecke's settled into their new home, finding comfort in the quiet of the Montana nights. As the couple nestled in bed, two cherished pets, a fluffy calico cat and a spirited Jack Russell Terrier named Pepe, burrowed in a cozy pile of warmth and companionship.

As they drifted to sleep, a distinct sound pierced the tranquility of night: a dog drinking from a dish, tags gently tapping against the ceramic bowl. John, half asleep, reached out to feel for Pep. His fingers encountered a warm bundle where Pepe was gently snoring. He opened one eye and saw the cat curled up beside them, determining that the drinking of neither pet was the source of the sound. The tapping continued, each metallic chime echoing through the house.

Wild-eyed and bewildered, the family of four sat up in bed, illuminated by the soft glow of moonlight. Josie cautiously peered over the bed's edge, her heart pounding, but nothing could be seen. Only the curious presence lingered in the air. Huddling under their blankets, they pulled them up around their shoulders, squeezing their eyes shut as they sought solace in each other's presence, the mysterious tapping sounds continuing in the background momentarily and then stopping still. The night was alive with a preternatural sensation, leaving them with more questions than answers and a lingering awareness that their new home held secrets they were only beginning to uncover.

Creole Cat

In the steamy summer of 1996, John and Josie ventured into the enchanting heart of New Orleans, a city steeped in history, mystery, and a touch of the supernatural. Their days were filled with the vibrant flavors of Creole cuisine, the rhythmic beats of jazz spilling from smoky clubs, and the thrill of fishing for redfish and stripers in the murky bayous. They explored the land's rich heritage, harvesting sugarcane from verdant fields and stepping back in time at a cotton plantation where echoes of the past still lingered in the air.

Saturday afternoon, their journey led them to a historic plantation, where they joined a bustling tour group eager to unravel the tales of days gone by. As the guide regaled them with stories of culinary traditions from a bygone era, the group huddled in the plantation's kitchen. The air was heavy with the scents of spices and simmering dishes, and the walls seemed to whisper secrets of times long past.

In this kitchen, among the clatter of pans and the storytelling, Josie felt a gentle presence brushing against her legs. Surprised, she looked down, expecting to find a friendly feline seeking comfort in her company. Most cats shied away from strangers, making her feel somewhat unique to be the chosen one.

With a soft smile, Josie leaned down to offer a scratch behind the kitty's ear. Her fingers extended toward the invisible furry form, but what met her touch was nothing but empty air. Her heart skipped a beat as her hair stood on edge, the sensation of phantom fur lingering on her fingertips.

In a final act of farewell, she felt the phantom cat's shoulder glide away from her and onto the next person in the group. A tail wrapped around her leg for a fleeting second, a spectral goodbye from her invisible feline friend. She looked around the crowd, her eyes wide with wonder. Everyone else remained oblivious, engrossed in the speaker's tales and the history surrounding them. Josie couldn't help but feel that she had crossed paths with a ghostly inhabitant of the plantation, a feline spirit from times passed, still yearning for a human touch. The experience left her with a sense of the mystical and a deeper connection to the enigmatic allure of New Orleans, where history and the supernatural danced together in a sultry, timeless embrace.

UFOs and Ghostly Whispers at Parson Montana Ranch

In the early 1930s, a married couple, Mr. and Mrs. Mabel Parson, had a little boy named Georgie who lived on a homestead. A local boy, Bill Cullinan, worked on this farm, helping build a large garden during the "Dirty 30." Farming in Montana during the 1930s was deeply affected by the Great Depression and the Dust Bowl that occurred previously. Farmers faced economic hardships due to falling crop prices, reduced demand for farm products, and a lack of access to credit. Many struggled to make ends meet and faced foreclosure on their farms.

While working on their farm outside Glendive, Montana, a horse kicked little Georgie in the head, nearly killing him. He survived with a traumatic brain injury. Georgie never progressed past the mental age of six. He grew up but never left home. By the 1960s, his mother, Mabel, and father had passed away, leaving the property and their dependent without a caregiver.

In 1963, Bill Cullinan and his wife Alice bought the farm and unofficially adopted "Little Georgie" along with it. Georgie was older than Alice and Bill but still needed a guardian. When the mood arose, he was a good helping hand but often chose to play and spend leisure time. Bill and Alice settled in with their bustling brood: Linda, Pat, Bob, Billy, and Sharon.

Alice's brother, John, lived just down the road with his wife, Eloise. She and Alice became the dearest of friends. John and Eloise had children of their own: Carolyn, Marie, Susan, John Jr., Jim, and Kathy. The two families worked and played together and had spooky encounters on multiple occasions.

When Bill and Alice first purchased the property, it had electricity but no running water. Bill and the neighbors worked cooperatively to channel the spring water and get it running under the house year-round so it would never freeze up, giving the family fresh water to utilize every day of the year.

One night, after getting moved in and settled, the entire family was sitting around the table eating supper when they heard a loud crash that sounded like glass breaking upstairs. They continued eating and discussed the noise. After some supposition, the family agreed that the prominent light fixture in the primary bedroom had fallen from the ceiling and shattered. They finished dinner, and Alice set the kids to clean the kitchen while she gathered the broom and dustpan to clean up the glass. She was surprised to find not only were the fixtures still hanging, but there was no glass anywhere upstairs to be found. They never found that broken glass in the thirty years they resided in that farmhouse.

Once, Alice, Bill, and the kids were outside all day doing work on the farm. When they left in the morning, the house was tidy. The kitchen had an electric range and a wood-burning stove, and logs piled up high in the wood box for when they were needed for burning. When they returned in the evening, the wood was tossed all over the kitchen. The family questioned Georgie why he had done that, to which he replied that he hadn't. Unfortunately, it wasn't until that happened multiple times and when they were away that the family began to suspect that an active entity was living within their home's walls. Since this persnickety spirit didn't seem malicious, more of a busybody, the family began attributing the activity to Mabel, Georgie's mother, the previous homeowner.

Another morning, when the family was having breakfast around the table, one of the children noticed a pool of blood on the floor underneath the table. They could not find any injured animal or reason for blood to be on the floor. It was far more than a mouse or killing of a pest would leave behind, and they didn't know how long it had been there, but it hadn't dried up. It simply remained pooled as if it was freshly spilled. Alice mopped it up when they were done eating breakfast and continued with her day.

One evening, Alice put the kids to bed, cleaned up, and readied herself for bed while Bill dressed for his night shift at the railway. He worked from eleven at night to seven in the morning. He would take the truck at night and leave home around ten when Alice would go to bed.

She would read for a bit, say goodnight to the dog who slept on a pallet at the foot of the bed, then turn out the lights and go to sleep. Around 11:15, she heard someone stomping up the stairs. She sat up, turned on the light, thought Bill had car trouble on the way to work, and walked back home. She called out to her husband, but no one answered back. Alice heard the loud pounding for so many steps that whoever it was should have been up the staircase, but the sound continued.

She decided not to investigate. They did not have a phone, and Bill had their only vehicle. Sitting on the bed with the blankets pulled up around her chin, Alice considered her options. The sound stopped, and she called out for Bill again. No one answered. She reasoned that if it were Bill, he would come into the bedroom, and if it wasn't, she hoped that whatever it was never breached the landing as that's where she and all the children were sleeping.

She finally decided that she must have been hearing things. Turning the light back out, she lay down. After a few minutes, she listened to the sound again. She called to the children, asking if they were up. No answer. At this time, the puppy got up from his bed, growling deep in his throat. The dog, tail raised, walked cautiously to the doorway. He reached the door, looked out into the hall, and all his hair stood on end. He froze. Alice, growing bold, realized she must stand her ground.

"Listen, Ghost. I don't know if you're Mabel or who you are, but I've had enough!" She scolded in her strongest authoritarian voice. "We work very hard in this house and are sleeping, so you'd better quiet down now. You hear?"

She scolded the phantom fiercely from the safety of her bed. Deciding not to look into the hall, she called the dog to lay with her and left the light on for the entire night. Properly chastised, the stomping ceased. Eventually, she fell asleep. She told Bill all about it in the morning.

Another day, Bill and John, her brother-in-law who also worked for the railway, had been called to work to assist with a trainwreck. John's wife, Eloise, had come over with her children: Carolyn, Marie, Susan, John Jr., Jim, and Kathy. Additionally, there was another boy named Patrick who was estranged from his parents and staying with the Cullinans for the time being. Eloise had the idea for the ladies to attend a local auction. Alice agreed, and it was decided. They would go while the older girls, Marie and Susan, cooked supper and looked after the younger children.

Patrick was riding his motorcycle from the Cullinans to the neighbors through the coulee when he noticed a mysterious mist in the shape of an ominous figure rising from the ravine. He stopped dead in his tracks. After getting a good look, he jumped back on his bike and raced home. He got Pat, Alice, and Bill's boy to ride back with him. Patrick pointed out over the coulee and told Pat to look over there. When both boys saw the figure rise out of the wash shrouded in a mist, the boys squealed,

"Let's get the hell out of here!" Popping a wheelie, they rode that rear tire all the way home. They got home screeching hysterically about the ghost following them up the hill. The older girls didn't believe them, but the boys convinced them to leave supper cooking and come look out front.

The whole gaggle of kids went out to the porch and watched in disbelief as the figure very clearly floated up the hill, through the fence, and into the old horse trailer. Beyond the trailer was an old Northern Pacific bus the family used for traveling. The phantasm floated through the trailer and into the bus. Filing the bus with a mystic fog, they all began screaming when the bus started to honk, and every light in the bus began to flash. The children all ran inside the house, slamming the door closed. Dinner was all but forgotten. The children all huddled together until the mothers returned.

The ladies were headed to Eloise's but noticed the porch light at the Cullinans flashing wildly. The ladies presumed that the kids must need something and turned to head there. When they entered the home, every light was on, and the children were convinced that an evil spirit was stalking them just outside. The kids were tripping over each other to get nearer to their mothers, telling the story in a confused jumble about how the ghost followed the boys home from the gulley. The two women had never seen their children so frightened. Eloise took her children, and they went home.

Alice could do no amount of convincing to get her children to go to bed that night. Sharon was crying about how frightened they all were. Alice sensibly told her daughter that there are no such things as ghosts. Sharon told her, "Mother, when you see it. You believe it." All the kids, large and small, slept in their mother's bedroom. The little ones in the bed and big kids on the floor nearby. None of the children were willing to risk leaving their mother's side that night.

There was a downstairs room that the Cullinans called the music room because it was where the musical instruments were housed. There was an old leather sofa that the Parsons had left behind. One night, Pat got up in the middle of the night to use the restroom. He saw someone from the corner of his eye sitting on that couch. Pat was startled, knowing it was the middle of the night and no one should be up. Turning, he looked, and to his horror, he saw something so chilling he had difficulty describing it. He rubbed his eyes and blinked.

In the chair was the figure of a bloated man who was moving and floating like he was made of balloons. Pat, petrified, felt that it was undoubtedly evil. He leaned into the bathroom to pick up a shoe his sister had left on the floor to throw, but when he looked back, it was gone. Shaking, he used the restroom and ran back to bed. That vision haunted him for the rest of the year.

The big kids camped outside in the truck bed one summer night as they love to on clear, warm nights. They gathered blankets and lanterns. Alice and Bill smiled, hearing the kids laughing and goofing off into the early hours. Finally, they wore themselves out. One by one, they fell asleep. In the morning, they came back in for breakfast, saying they were onto their mother's tricks. When she asked what they were talking about, they said they knew she was under the truck, hitting the chassis and making those noises, trying to wake them up, but they teased back, saying that she couldn't scare them so easily.

"Do you think I could still crawl under that truck?" she asked them seriously. Then, the children looking at each other lost their good humor and went a little pale. It was some time before the kids asked to camp outside again.

Another visitor to the property was a government trapper, Jerry, who made fast friends with Bill and Alice's brother, John. Jerry frequented the area, conducting different animal surveys, and finally, Alice invited him not only to spend the night at their place but to bring his wife Patty and their little girl too. Alice told him for the girls to bring their pajamas so they could sleep at the Cullinans while Bill, John, and Jerry tromped the countryside trapping until the wee hours. The men had a fine time, and they all reconvened in the kitchen for breakfast come morning.

"Goodness, Alice. How early do you get up to start breakfast?" Patty asked.

"Whenever I wake up," Alice responded. "Usually around six. Why do you ask?"

"Well, that's funny," Patty replied. "We heard someone rummaging through the pantry, making quite the racket this morning around three."

"Oh!" Alice responded casually. "That was just our ghost."

"Alice!" Bill chided. "You're going to run our friends off." Bill teased, giving her a stern, half-teasing look. Everyone laughed, thinking that the couple was making a joke.

Over the summer, when a pair of sheep shearers were spending the night downstairs in the covered porch, they also reported hearing a ruckus in the pantry at about three in the morning. It was then that the family found that this occurrence happened pretty regularly, but they were too far away to hear. Many people who slept downstairs reported the very thing over the years.

Another boy, Niel, stayed with the Cullinans for a while. He was a runaway who was having trouble and needed shelter for a time. He was around the age of the older kids, and they had the best of times together. In the summertime, they would tack up the horses and go on midnight rides or, at other times, take the truck and drive the three miles to the mailbox and then to the four miles to the sheep camp, talking and laughing innocently.

One night, when all the teenagers and Georgie were cutting up at the campsite, they suddenly felt like someone was watching them. Getting quiet and looking around, they saw a mist that took the form of a man.

Without any discussion, the kids made a break for the truck. Starting it up and driving off, Sharon screamed,

"Wait! Wait for Georgie." Pat looked back to see that Georgie was running behind the truck. Unwilling to stop, the driver slowed down just long enough for Georgie to catch up and hop in the bed. Once everyone was onboard, the kids sped home like a demon was chasing them.

There was another time when Eloise was taking her children, nephew, and niece to town when a floating light was trailing them. It was blinding bright, shining right in her mirror. After some time, Eloise stomped the gas to get ahead of it. Much to her surprise, it sped up and hovered right next to her, and she could see it was nothing of this world. Thinking it was unwise to meddle with an unidentified flying object, she slowed, wanting it to go on its way, but the object slowed and followed right next to her. This went on for some time until it finally darted off across the field and out of sight. When she went over to Alice and Bill's the next day. She told them all about it. Bill said he'd had the same experience.

Later that summer, some cattle rustlers on the ranch described something similar. At first, they thought someone was following them in another vehicle, but soon they realized that this thing was floating and not following the road, and suddenly, as quick as it appeared, it was back into the sky and too far away to see. They said their neighbor, Ray Osbey, was riding out in the winter pasture and came upon a perfectly round spot in which the snow was melted as something hot had just been there before he went over the hill. There were no tracks or any indication of how it left the scene other than to fly directly up.

There was a different incident where Alice was home alone and got the spookiest feeling of being watched. She stopped and prayed aloud.

"Lord, if we're being haunted, let me get a look at this thing." She opened her eyes, expecting to come face to face with her tormentor. However, looking around, she failed to see a thing. She was relieved but remained curious.

1978 Alice, Bill, Jimmy, Sharon, and Bob were in the front of the house. They heard a soft whirring noise outside. They went out on the front porch and looked down by the big draw. There, they saw a flying saucer not far off the ground. It seemed to be purring up and down. It had colored lights blinking all over the shell. A moment later, it shot up into the sky.

Alice's neighbor, Harriet Ames, described an event in 1967 on the highway coming home from Circle to Glendive on the other side of Lindsey. The road was a two-lane highway with a fence on either side. She was driving with her daughter, and a light came alongside her vehicle on the left. It was so fast she couldn't see it clearly. It passed over them, and suddenly, there was a big puff of smoke to the right of the road. She stopped and looked and saw a large circle of burnt grass and ashes. She didn't know what it was, but it seemed to have crashed and combusted, completely vaporizing.

Her husband, Stanley, and his brother, Everett, also saw strange lights in 1988 in two separate incidents. They two were working late in Baker. They drove back from Wibeaux, ten miles out of Glendive, around 2 am. They saw a bright light off to the side, less than two miles away. It hung there lit up. They stopped, and it stopped. It seemed to be hovering over the badlands of Glendive for about 30 minutes.

Six or eight years later, they were driving at 3 am. They saw a flying object they initially thought might be a helicopter, but it was too close and silent. It was a still night, hovering over them silently for five or ten minutes. Abruptly, it shot directly up and was gone. It was too bright to see. When it rose up and shone down on the city, it lit up the whole town with a bright white light. He said when his sister came from Sidney to Glendive, there was more than one account in which a saucer would hover along, keep up with pickup, and then zip away.

Back on the Parson Ranch, another day just after dinner, the noon meal, Bill told the family to stack the dishes in the sink and save the washing for later because he needed everyone's help gathering horses from the pasture. The family piled into the truck, including Georgie. They worked all afternoon gathering the herd and securing the wild horses in the paddock for breaking.

When they returned that evening, the dishes were scattered all over the floor, with dog food piled on top. They all walked around the kitchen with their hair standing on end. When they entered the living room, all the furniture had been tipped over. Putting her hands on her hips in exasperation, Alice huffed.

"Mabel's been at work here."

"Stop saying that!" Bill ordered his wife. "You're going to scare yourself and then get the wild idea that you want to move."

"I'm not moving," Alice snorted. "This is my home. I'm not leaving." And to this day. She never has.

There came a day when Georgie packed up his wagon and went to play in the pasture as he often did and never returned. When he went missing past supper time, the family split up, everyone looking for him. His body was found near his little wagon, but dear old Georgie was no longer there. The doctors never expected him to live long after his childhood accident and considered every day of adulthood a gift. The doctors surmised he had had an aneurysm.

He was playing, and before he knew it, he just slipped away. The family took care of him respectfully and held a service for him. For some reason, there didn't seem to be any disturbances after Georgie's passing. Some think the entity was his mother trying to look out for him until he could join her among the clouds.

Ultimately, the Cullinan family's decades-long coexistence with the unexplained phenomena surrounding their home, known as the Parson Ranch, left them with remarkable stories. From the playful but unsettling antics of a mysterious presence to the encounters with unidentified flying objects, their lives were intertwined with the unfathomable. Their beloved family member, Georgie, defied the odds with each passing day, leaving them with sadness and a newfound peace as the peculiar occurrences seemed to subside. The Cullinans' home was where the boundaries of reality blurred, and they faced the unknown with courage, resilience, and a touch of humor. It was a place where the past, present, and otherworldly converged, creating a legacy of stories that would continue to intrigue and mystify future generations.

Lady of Light

In the heart of a bustling Tyson Factory, amid the clang of machinery and the roar of industrial activity, Mario Villareal, son of Terri, a dedicated family man, toiled away. It was a place where the hum of countless conveyor belts seemed to drown out the world, a relentless cacophony that mirrored the chaos of life. Mario was going through a harrowing divorce. The burdens of separation weighed down his heart.

One night, exhausted by his duties on the floor, Mario's world shifted. A radiant, blinding light encircled him. An otherworldly presence descended upon the factory. Squinting against the brilliance, his mouth went dry, and his heart racing. A spirit materialized before him, a protector from beyond ethereal light. She regarded Mario with eyes that held a wisdom beyond mortal comprehension. Reaching out, she spoke.

"You see the light," she resonated, her voice a haunting echo within him. Mario, stunned by the luminous presence, replied.

"Yes, but I see darkness too." His admission hung in the air, heavy with the weight of turmoil. The protector's expression shifted from one of serenity to grave concern. A palpable chill swept through the factory as Mario's words hung over them, the machinery's ambient noise fading into silence. The atmosphere of the factory seemed to sense the unnatural presence. A hushed tension filled the room.

Oblivious to the celestial encounter unfolding beside them, Mario's coworkers continued their work methodically. The messenger's eyes bore into Mario's soul as if peering through the layers of his pain. Her whisper sent a shiver down his spine.

"Beware the darkness that lingers, for it seeks to consume you." With those haunting words, she vanished into the radiant light, leaving Mario alone in the factory, forever changed by the encounter.

From that day forward, Mario could never forget the luminous apparition that visited him. The workshop's relentless noise seemed to echo the angelic presence, a reminder of the darkness that threatened to engulf his soul. The protector's words reverberated in his mind, a chilling prophecy of the trials ahead, as Mario wrestled with forces of light and dark that swirled within and around him.

Echoes of Cosmic Reminiscence

This is an honest and accurate recollection of a man living on Earth. The prelude to his earthly existence unfolded in John's memory. He retained vague recollections of existing in enigmatic realms, accompanied by companions whose cosmic essence resembled stardust. Together, they dwelled within a collective consciousness, an ethereal congregation of souls.

Among them stood an unfathomable presence. John hesitated, voicing reluctance about the impending journey into an unfamiliar body. He vividly recalled his protestations, his plea not to return to Earth, but the entity assured him that this would mark his final voyage to the planet. Reflecting on these memories, John couldn't shake the feeling that the cycle of rebirth might lead to diverse forms of existence, whether as a human, an animal, or an alien entity in another celestial body. These inklings hinted that his previous life might not have been human. He was confident he had undergone this process countless times. In one of his prior human lives, he had endured a wretched existence akin to an exploited individual, perhaps an enslaved person, with the memories of those times only leaving him with a profound sense of despair.

Abruptly, brilliant and intimidating luminescence engulfed him. The sterile hospital room materialized in his mind's eye in intricate detail, a map carved into his memory. John's reaction was astonished discomfort; the newfound physicality of his being was overwhelming. The relentless brightness of his surroundings induced fear. His nascent thoughts swirled a maelstrom of bewilderment.

Like the swift descent from the cosmos, he found himself cradled, his new body alien. Desperation coursed through him as he yearned to communicate, yet he could only articulate his distress through inconsolable cries. Simple situations, like needing a drink, emphasized the limitations of his infantile body as he waited to have his needs understood. Painfully apparent, human embodiment brought an array of constraints, foremost among them the inability to voice one's desires, a frustrating revelation in this new existence.

In this prison, John grappled with profound intuition, pondering the grand cycle of rebirth, entertaining thoughts of past lives as creatures of Earth and otherworldly realms. He resented his new body, unsophisticated and uncontrollable. He despised the years it would take to master. Gnawing hunger and the discomfort of soiled diapers only exacerbated his frustration.

His crib, once a prison, transformed into a challenging puzzle. A small board concealed a hole in the base, offering a glimmer of iance and freedom. Shifting that board became his act of rebellion, a daring crawl to newfound liberty, inevitably met with parental consternation. Their emotional outbursts bewildered him, an early thought that human emotions were beyond his comprehension.

As John journeyed through human infancy, frustration remained a constant companion, driving his relentless pursuit of self-mastery. His existence was a complex tapestry of cosmic nostalgia and earthly turmoil, an ever-evolving narrative.

As time flowed, John learned to walk, though slow and cumbersome. Each step is an affront to his innate desire for autonomy. He was angered by the lack of control and frustrated by the reliance on others for assistance.

John couldn't ascertain the duration of this early stage of his life, but he was confident it followed a timeline of normal human development. Unremarkable was his birth to his family. Living on a farm in the 1950s, his mother often worked in the fields. His primary carers were his sisters, Diane and Judy. However, often preoccupied, he left John to his own devices.

Growing up, John reached a significant milestone at three when an unforgettable incident occurred. While outdoors with sister Sue, wielding shovels in the dirt, held a claw hammer. They were crafting miniature roads for their toy cars and trucks. Sue's constant interference provoked him as she reached into his path to move the dirt.

Despite warnings, she persisted. In a moment of exasperation, John swung the hammer. Her fingers were severed cleanly. Sue fled, crying and bleeding, to their house, setting off a flurry of panic among the adults. Swiftly, she was hospitalized, her fingers reattached. John's mind was uncomprehending the gravity of the situation and remained unfazed by the commotion.

Empathy was an elusive concept for John during those early years. He didn't lack empathy but didn't yet understand it. His own emotions remained a puzzle, let alone those of others. He fondly recalled his father reading stories as he developed and improved his communication skills. The concept of books and storytelling fascinated him, making him wonder whether these experiences were new and unusual compared to his previous existence.

Growing older and finding his voice, John cherished the evenings when his father, Ollie, read him stories. It was a time when the world transformed into a realm of wonder and sensory delight. In the dimly lit room, the scent of old books and the warmth of a well-worn armchair created an atmosphere of storytelling magic. John's anticipation would mount as his father's voice, rich with emotion, filled the air. The tales his father read were like hidden treasures, promising adventures yet to be discovered.

Within their story-filled pages, books held an enchantment that John couldn't resist. They transported him to a place beyond his earthly origins, where tales were born anew. The sensation of paper beneath his tiny fingers, the illustrations that danced before his eyes, all paled compared to the stories that unfolded in his mind. As his father read, John's friends, the beloved characters, came to life, puppeteering captivating scenarios. The cadence of his father's voice, combined with the sensory experience, created a delightful symphony.

Among the many stories, the folktales of Briar Wolf, Bowser the Hound, and Briar Fox, known as the "Uncle Remus" stories by Joel Chandler Harris, held a special place in John's memory. These narratives breathed life into animal characters, endowing them with traits mirroring those of humans. Br'er Rabbit, in particular, captured John's heart with his cunning wit and humor. His escapades, always one step ahead of his adversaries, showcased the power of clever thinking.

One story, imprinted indelibly in John's mind, featured Br'er Rabbit's escape from Br'er Fox through reverse psychology, tricking his foe into throwing him into a briar patch. Bowser the Hound, portrayed as fierce and persistent, was repeatedly outwitted by Br'er Rabbit, leaving young John laughing wildly. These stories weren't just amusing. They imparted valuable life lessons about wit, resourcefulness, and the art of turning adversity into advantage.

Fear became a potent motivator and catalyst for learning and personal growth in John's evolving world. While John initially lacked fear in his early youth, he grew to understand its vital role in one's journey. He believed that some would never grasp life's profound lessons without it. Fear could awaken latent potential, guiding individuals toward growth and enlightenment. In shaping human behavior and knowledge acquisition, fear played a pivotal role. Its absence might render some oblivious to life's profound lessons, making it a powerful motivator that compels individuals to embrace life's complexities.

John was funneled into the public education system as his toddlerhood was eclipsed. He couldn't help but feel repelled by what he perceived as a relentless bombardment of mundane information and interactions with people he considered dull. This experience left him feeling beaten down and disillusioned, a stark contrast to the wonder and excitement he had felt during his father's storytelling sessions. John's innate curiosity and affinity for books and stories remained steadfast despite this displeasure. As John developed and explored, consuming books of all types by the hundreds, then thousands, he traveled and worked all over the nation and overseas, studying humankind and scrutinizing various cultures and beliefs.

He acknowledged the intrinsic value of religion and its susceptibility to corruption, viewing it as a powerful source of faith stemming from the tangible existence of the church. In his view, angels, demons, and spiritual entities were as substantial as human belief made them.

The more people collectively believed in these entities, the more credence they held. In the complex tapestry of human thought, John found no absolute truths, only beliefs that grew stronger with followers. In retrospect, John believed that God was a multifaceted concept molded by human ideas and intertwined with the essence of existence. He thought of humans as creators of god, each possessing a divine spark within, proof of humans living in a matrix where perception and collective consciousness shaped reality, with god transcending new-age ideas.

John expressed skepticism regarding organized religion. He acknowledged the church's great value in providing faith and comfort to its believers but questioned its profit-driven motives. The church had evolved into a business entity, compromising its role as a spiritual guide. Despite corruption within the church, John believed that the faith and peace of mind it offered its followers still held intrinsic value. John's perspective on spirituality was grounded in the idea that human beliefs could shape their reality. While recognizing organized religions' flaws, he believed they were fallible human interpretations strengthened by collective faith.

Nirvana, a concept he explored deeply, held profound spiritual significance in Buddhism and Hinduism. It represented the ultimate goal of spiritual practice, the cessation of suffering, and liberation from the cycle of birth, death, and rebirth. Achieving nirvana meant a state of perfect peace and enlightenment. John believed such concepts hinted at an interstellar odyssey, where consciousness unfolded across various dimensions, unveiling the intricate tapestry of existence.

An ever-evolving battle between a fight for survival and an understanding of spirituality, existence, and the role of fear in human development marked John's journey through life. He continued to question the nature of reality, drawing from his early memories and experiences to shape his unique perspective on the world. In his ongoing quest for enlightenment and oneness, John found himself on a path of self-discovery that transcended the boundaries of conventional thought.

He contemplated fear's significance as a catalyst for learning, its role in shaping human destinies, and the profound concepts of nirvana in Buddhism and Hinduism. His perceptions of divinity evolved, viewing god as a reflection of human belief and pieces of ourselves, a malleable concept shaped by collective faith. This led him to ponder that human lived in a matrix, where human perception and collective consciousness sculpt reality. He believed that unity and transcendence held humanity's ultimate purpose—elusive, enigmatic, and ever-evolving.

Man Bygone

In the quiet countryside in the 1950s, where the rolling hills met the endless fields, John and his family had settled near the old homeplace. He was a toddler who became a curious child with a surreal connection to the past. Once, when they were driving down an old country road a few counties over, little John pointed out a window and began talking about how the house burned down. He told his family with startling precision where each charred beam and crumbled brick lay in the remains of the once-standing house. To everyone's amazement, he claimed he had lived there in a lifelong one that belonged to another era.

With wide-eyed wonder, John described the building with an accurate familiarity. He spoke of its inhabitants, his family of yesteryear, people who had long since departed from this world but remained vivid in his memory. To his sisters, Sue and Judy, he recounted stories on more than one occasion that seemed to defy the boundaries of time.

He told them about the construction of the house—the creaking wooden floors, the faded wallpaper that whispered of bygone days, and the way the sunlight filtered through dusty windows, casting ethereal patterns on the worn rugs. John painted a picture of his life as another man, there in times past, describing his experience walking in the shoes of those who dwelt within those weathered walls.

Listening to his mesmerizing tales, the family was transported to another era, feeling the weight of history pressing upon them. John's unspeakable connection to the past was a mystery that left them in awe, forever bound by the ties of a homeplace with secrets and stories only he seemed to remember.

Phantom of the Silage

In July of the 1960s, young John Lorbiecke found himself in the company of the Nelson kids, who lived a mile away. Their playful escapade led them down a winding road, where they stumbled upon a sight that would etch itself into their memories. Amidst the verdant fields, an array of mysterious equipment loomed, a forbidden playground into which they were forbidden to venture, fraught with danger. The air they breathed was tainted with hazardous gas, including the treacherous hydrogen sulfide, a colorless, poisonous, corrosive, and flammable gas. Its foul odor, reminiscent of rotten eggs, lingered ominously around them.

Storm clouds overhead cast threatening shadows as they played in the hazardous silage pit. Oblivious to the dangers, they set off journeying homeward, their path taking them up and down looming hills. It was then, in the midst of the inclement weather, that a sensation of dread crept over them. Alongside their procession came an inexplicable phenomenon—a flaming ball of light, radiant and white-hot, yet strangely devoid of discernible heat. Suspended a few feet above the Earth, it glided effortlessly, casting an otherworldly glow upon their astonished faces.

Their faces flushed with frightened wonder as the unfathomable orb descended closely, then drifted down the road and up the hill, defying the laws of physics as they knew them. Spellbound, they watched the mysterious ball until it vanished into the night. None of them can fathom the nature of the extraordinary spectacle that had crossed their path. An encounter with the unexplained that would plague their memories and stoke the flames of curiosity within them for a lifetime.

Abandoned House Thriller

When he was a teenager, John's cousin Craig picked him up along with his brother Dan and sister Sue. With nothing to do and nowhere to go, the kids snooped around an abandoned house they suspected to be haunted. Poking about in the dark where they shouldn't, every creak or groan of the old house settling frightened them. Sue suggested they leave for the third time as an ominous chill fell over the group. Silenced, their intuitions told them they were no longer alone. Behind them, in the pantry, old cans fell without provocation. They froze. A strange gust went through the house and out front, where Craig's truck was parked. Sue grabbed Dan's arm in alarm as he headed after it.

Just then, the truck lights flickered once on and then off. All four kids standing in the doorway watched the truck in disbelief. Next, the vehicle began to wildly rock back and forth as if a two-ton steer was being roped in the truck bed. Swearing all the tires would get popped, Craig ran outside toward his vehicle, fists balled up with no plan. As soon as he reached the truck and unlatched the door, the rocking ceased, and the heavy presence that seemed to be with them evaporated. With the threat gone, they jumped in the truck and went home, desperate to escape the creepy house.

Starry Night

In the autumn of 1982, John Lorbiecke and his coworker Rocky were toiling late into the crisp night for an oil company. Their task was a precarious mission to blow out a line that had succumbed to the unforgiving grip of frost. Sun dipping below the horizon cast long shadows across the remote field. John assumed his position at the lonely outpost while Rocky remained at the distant plant.

The chill in the air was palpable. The night was laden with stillness, broken only by the distant hum of industrial machinery. The world held its breath, anticipating the strange events unfolding. In the dimming light of dusk, John's eyes scanned the expansive sky, searching for any sign of change, when suddenly, a shimmering light pierced the heavens.

It appeared as an elongated star, a dark silver luminary that defied explanation. There was no roar of engines, no drone of aircraft. It traversed the sky in a silent, dreamlike dance. With bated breath, John watched in awe as this curious celestial traveler glided gracefully from one end of the horizon to the other, completing its astonishing journey in seconds.

The air, electrified with wonder and trepidation, John stood alone in the lonely night, bearing witness to a phenomenon that defied the laws of conventional understanding. The memory of that night would remain forever in his thoughts, an enduring testament to the mysteries that lurk beyond the frame of our familiarity.

Dawn Departure

In the pre-dawn stillness of the farm, young Vance Revell, just a boy, had a task that he had performed countless times before. Grandma had instructed him to fetch his uncle for breakfast, a daily ritual on their rural homestead. As the rooster's distant crow announced impending daybreak, Vance set out on his mission.

Cradled among the fields and pastures, the farmhouse bore witness to generations of early risers. Life on the farm demanded it; there were cows to be milked, fields to be tended, and chores too impatient to wait for the sun. Vance was accustomed to the rhythm of these mornings, but today was different. Darkness blanketing the land, Vance ventured out into the hushed cool air. Breath hanging like ghostly mist, he walked toward the great barn, a sentinel of countless memories.

"Uncle!" Vance called out, his voice puncturing the tranquility. There was no response. Not a rustle, not a murmur. The boy's steps faltered as he approached his uncle's room. And just like that, things changed. Vance watched, breathless in the shadows, as a radiant ball of energy, as bright as the morning sun, emerged from his great uncle's chest. It lingered transfixed, a luminous orb of iridescent colors, before gently expanding, its edges blending into the indigo canvas of the sky.

Bewilderment coursed throughout him. He stumbled back, his eyes locked on the empyrean spectacle unfolding before him. This was no prosaic occurrence, no trick of the dawn's early light. It was something far more profound which defied explanation.

Grandma's voice broke through Vance's shock. She had followed him, her face a weathered mask of somber wisdom.

"That's his soul," she said, her words carrying the weight of generations. "His spirit leaving this world after death." Her eyes glimmered as she nodded farewell to her dear son. The realization descended upon Vance like a lightning bolt. He watched, eyes glistening, as the radiant energy dispersed into the atmosphere, joining the ever-expanding tapestry of the universe.

In that fleeting moment, Vance had witnessed something sacred, a connection to the mysteries of life and death that had played out on this land for centuries. The farm, his family, and the timeless rituals of their existence were now imbued with a profound depth, a reminder that the land held secrets far older and grander than they could ever fathom.

Super Charger Bee vs. Luminous Orb

In the fall of 1978, Vance Revell, now a young man, his mother, younger brother, and a friend named Jay, embarked on a journey from Montana to Washington State. Their route led them through the winding, mountainous terrain of Interstate 90 near Helena. Unbeknownst to them, this trip would become a bizarre experience imprinted in their minds.

Their mode of transportation was Vance's pride and joy. She was a green and black pinstriped 1971 Dodge Charger Super Bee, a beast equipped with a formidable 440 Magnum engine and a 4-speed overdrive transmission. Vance reveled in the power of the machine as he pushed it beyond 100 miles per hour on the open road, the engine's roar harmonizing with the wind. The flirtation between machine and road was interrupted when the passengers noticed an oddity in the rearview mirror. There, tailing them at an incredible speed, was a fascinating sight: an orange, glowing sphere. It trailed them in an unwavering shadow, casting a disturbing glow on the highway.

Curiosity mingled with fear as the mile markers flew by. The strange orb continued pursuit. Vance's foot stroked the accelerator, pushing the Charger past 160 miles per hour. The ball of light remained in pursuit, an unnatural, relentless presence. Vance and his family couldn't make sense of what they were witnessing. How could an object maintain such astonishing speed? Doubts gnawed at them, and malaise clenched the pits of their stomachs.

Panic mounted when the radiant orb drew closer with a sudden burst of acceleration, revealing its immense size, 50 to 100 feet across. It cast an orange-yellow hue on the surroundings, illuminating the night like an ungodly sun. Frantically, Vance pushed the Charger to its limits, his heart in overdrive. He prayed for an escape from this conundrum. The incandescent globe assessed them, airborne just behind as if mocking their apprehension.

In an electrifying moment, it happened. The colossal orb veered sharply to the left and ascended into the sky, disappearing into the darkness instantaneously. Vance's mother, overwhelmed by the event, sobbed inconsolably. They had been scrutinized and examined by something beyond comprehension that violated our nature's laws. As they continued their journey, shaken but alive, the group couldn't help but wonder about the mysterious rendezvous. What had they witnessed that night on the Montana highway? The answers evaded them, shrouded in mystery, a memory of suspense they would not soon forget.

Cherub's Flight

Vance Revell's connection with his grandmother was unique, a bond that transcended generations and was rooted in something more profound than a blood bond. His grandmother possessed a gift, a psychic insight passed down their lineage. It was a gift that came at a high cost, a burden of supernatural knowledge that weighed on her soul. Their lives intersected in a small, cozy farmhouse that had seen the passage of many seasons. Vance's infant daughter, only two months old, lay cradled in his arms. He gazed upon her cherubic face, her eyes a canvas of innocent wonder. His heart swelled with love, an indescribable tenderness for the fragile life he held in his arms.

"Perfect," he whispered, his voice filled with pride and adoration as she grasped his rugged hands with her tiny pink fingers. He couldn't fathom a more wonderful creation than his baby girl.

His grandmother, seated across from him in her worn armchair, wore a somber expression that betrayed the heaviness of her heart. Her eyes, aged and wise, bore witness to a world unseen. With a sigh that carried the weight of centuries, she uttered words that pierced the joyous moment like a blade.

"She is very beautiful," his grandmother agreed. Frowning, she went on. "It's a shame she won't survive," she murmured, her voice laced with sorrow and a knowing that induced a shutter in Vance.

He recoiled, protective instincts surfacing. "What a heartless thing to say," he bit back, voice anger tinged at the cruelty of her words. "How could anyone speak such a fate for a helpless child?" His nerves wavered, knowing this old woman didn't make frightening claims out of malice. She hung her head, knowing she'd revealed too much.

The day grew late. Memory of the vexing conversation faded as Vance and his family settled into their routines. The grange resonated with the quiet hum of everyday life.

The next morning, the sun bathed the world in gentle warmth. Vance woke, mindful of his morning chores. His first order of business was to peek in on the baby. In one moment, his good morning kiss turned into an unimaginable nightmare. His infant daughter, his beloved angel, lay blue and motionless in her crib. She had passed away in her sleep. Her life extinguished before it had truly begun at nine weeks of life.

Vance cradled her lifeless form, grief-stricken. Sorrow consumed him, and in the depths of his despair, his grandmother's words replayed in his memory, uttered with a prescience that defied reason. He never asked his grandmother how she had known, for the answer would have been more than he could bear. She carried the weight of supernatural knowledge, a burden that allowed her to glimpse into the tapestry of fate but also condemned her to the anguish of foreseeing unpreventable tragedies.

Vance and his grandmother shared a connection forged by the mysteries of life and death, where love and agony danced an eternal waltz. This connection bound them in a profound, haunting embrace.

Bounty Hunter Immortal

By the summer of 1981, Vance had become a legendary figure in the world of bounty hunting. At 32 years old, he was a veteran of the hunt, renowned for his uncanny ability to sense true evil, a skill honed under the watchful guidance of his grandmother. He was no ordinary huntsman; he pursued only the most sinister criminals whose auras radiated a dark, malignant presence.

Vance was embroiled in a perilous mission one afternoon. A shady man with an unsettling aura had reached out to him, a request to retrieve a stash of dynamite from a forsaken job site deep in the desolation of North Dakota, far from the comforts of civilization, buried amidst dirt roads north of Beach. With reservation evoked by an ominous feeling, he reluctantly took the job.

Led by his instincts and fortified by his grandmother's lessons, Vance ventured ahead of the seedy character. But as he forged ahead, a pervasive feeling crawled up his spine, a foreboding that whispered of danger. Realizing an attack was imminent, he ducked and dove for cover.

The assailant struck, shooting Vance point-blank through the skull and shoulder. As he ducked behind a bush, Vance heard more bullets slicing through the air just past him. Hot stings prickled his senses. He surged with adrenaline. In shock, his instincts had saved him once again. He had evaded death's cold embrace, although not without fatal wounds. Blood poured from his eyes and ears as he huddled behind a makeshift refuge, a relentless spirit gathering strength for what lay ahead.

Heart pulsing with fury, Vance pursued the attacker, an avenging force fueled by a desire for justice. He closed in, tackling the man to the ground, unforgiving. A knife glinted in his hand, a weapon of retribution. Swiftly, mercilessly, he slid the blade into the man's throat and held it, silencing his adversary.

With the wounded man at his mercy, Vance, holding the knife precariously, compelled the man to drive him to the nearest hospital, an agonizing hour-long journey, the knife still protruding from his throat. A chilling threat hung in the air: Vance's vow to ensure his survival. He explained to his attacker-turned-transporter that the man's decapitation would be his last and final act if he lost consciousness before they arrived at the hospital.

The two arrived at Saint Alexius Health Dickinson Medical Center. Vance's identity was shrouded in secrecy. The staff suspected him of being a mob hit victim and guarded his presence fiercely, refusing to divulge any information about his hospitalization.

Meanwhile, Vance's grandmother, residing 300 miles away in Stanley, North Dakota, felt an unsettling intuition that her beloved grandson was in dire straits. Driven by instinct, she journeyed to find him. Arriving at the correct hospital, the staff was mystified when she showed proof of her identity and asked for him by name.

"How did you know he was here?" they asked suspiciously. Her response was simple yet laden with power.

"I just knew." In this extraordinary convergence of danger and intuition, Vance's grandmother had transcended the boundaries of time and distance to stand steadfastly by her wounded grandson's side. It was a testament to their unfettered bond, a connection that defied explanation and endured through the darkest of trials.

Lechuza of Victoria

When Teresa Flores, daughter of Julie Aguayo, was a teen living in Victoria, Texas, she argued with a family member and, full of angst, stormed out and down a country road to take a walk, clearing her head. Replaying the conflict within her mind, she was walking down the street impartial to her surroundings. She was startled to attention by a pair of giant wings flapping overhead. The colossal bird flew over her head and landed in the field.

At full attention, Teresa stopped, peering into the grass to observe the creature. What stood up unfolding from the tall grass was a tall, thin woman dressed all in black with stringy dark hair hanging down to her knees. Gripped in a cold sweat, she blinked, questioning what she had just seen. Looking straight at her, the woman began to whistle.

Without thinking, Teresa began to approach the creature. Closer and closer, she ventured, hearing the whistling more loudly. As she grew very near, the woman crouched down, and suddenly, a black bird took flight from where she was standing. Stunned in amazement, the creature circled Teresa once, twice, shrieked an ear-piercing cry, and flew off into the horizon. Frightened, she quickly made her way back home.

The Joke's on You

When Teresa was younger, her brother Fidel was known for being a bit of a prankster. Fidel and his girlfriend were visiting his mother's house. Teresa was getting ready to go out, and Fidel decided to sneak into her car and frighten her. Hunkering down, he waited for his sister. After sitting in a cramped position, he became restless and looked around to see if he could spot her coming outside. Fidel stretched up and peered into the rearview mirror and was shocked to see an ominous black figure sitting in the backseat watching him. He was consumed with the idea that this dark figure was some harbinger of death and that someone in that home would soon die. Less than one week later, his mother, Julie, passed away. The sight of that grim reaper is seared into his mind to this day.

Lost Soul of Nahum

After getting married and moving into her home, Teresa got a call from her Aunt Terri. She said a group of men were looking for work at the train station, who had just arrived from Vera Cruz, Mexico. Laborers often came to Texas looking for job opportunities for various reasons, their journeys influenced by economic factors, limited job opportunities, and income disparities. The wage gap between Mexico and the United States is significant. In some parts of Mexico, concerns about violence motivate individuals to seek safety and stability in the US. Their voyages often involve various challenges and risks. Still, the potential for improved economic prospects and a better quality of life in the United States remains a powerful incentive for many individuals and families.

It so happened that Teresa's brother-in-law, owned a hotel, was looking to hire a few hard-working men. When Teresa and her husband, Marcos, arrived at the station, a timid young man named Nahum said he was skilled and accepted any short-term job offers. Eyes darting back and forth, the boy admitted he feared he'd made a mistake and hoped they would help him get back home. The couple agreed to give him work and shelter for two weeks so he could have a safe place to stay and acquire the funds to buy a return ticket.

Although odd, Nahum worked hard at the hotel, and the family took measures to make him feel welcome and comfortable. Two weeks passed, then four, and Nahum's behavior grew concerning. One afternoon, Teresa planned to go to the mall to do some shopping. She told him about it and asked if he wanted to come along. Restless, he agreed.

She pursued a few specific items when they got to the shopping strip. Nahum became agitated. He told her in Spanish that he thought people were looking at him. She hadn't noticed anyone in particular staring at him and tried to put him at ease. When she supportively reached for his arm, he yanked away and yelled at her never to look him in the eyes.

Startled and alarmed, she cut her shopping trip short and went directly home. Teresa spoke to Marcos in private. She told him what happened and expressed that she no longer felt safe. They agreed that Nahum must leave. That night, after dinner, the couple sat him down to tell him they could no longer harbor him. They thanked him for his good work at the hotel but pointed out that the tile he was laying was finished. That meant his job, which had stretched twice as long as expected at the hotel, was now over. A little disgruntled, he offered to leave at first light.

Knowing that he now had the money to buy a train ticket but was too late to buy a ticket that night, they agreed that leaving the next morning would be best. As they bid him goodnight, he said he needed to speak to his "bruja." They were familiar with the concept. Although brujeria can indicate dark magic or malicious works, it most often includes works of benign guidance or healing.

Brujería, or witchcraft, is a complex, multifaceted aspect of culture that combines elements of indigenous beliefs, catholicism, and folk traditions. The craft varies among individuals and communities in views and practices. Brujería practitioners are sought after for protection and cleansing rituals believed to remove negative energies, curses, and hexes or to restore balance and well-being.

Witchdoctors hold respected positions within communities as spiritual leaders and healers, often vital in providing emotional and psychological support to those seeking assistance. Brujería reflects a syncretic blend of indigenous traditions, particularly those of the Nahua people and Spanish catholicism. This is evident through incorporating indigenous deities, catholic saints, and religious symbols into brujería practices. The use of herbs and natural remedies is a common feature of brujería. It may prepare herbal potions, teas, or ointments for various purposes, including healing, protection, and divination, such as reading cards, interpreting dreams, or using objects like candles, crystals, and mirrors for scrying. Magic is also an integral part of brujería, with practitioners performing rituals and spells for various purposes, including love, prosperity, and protection. Many brujos and brujas maintain altars in their homes or places of practice. These altars typically feature images of saints, candles, incense, and offerings like flowers, fruit, and food items and are used for prayer, ceremonies, and offerings to spiritual entities. Brujería practices may involve chanting, drumming, and dancing during specific times of the year or with religious holidays and festivals.

Despite its prevalence, brujería is sometimes viewed with skepticism or stigmatized by mainstream society. As a result, many practitioners keep their beliefs and practices private. It's important to approach discussions of brujería with cultural sensitivity and respect for the beliefs and practices of the individuals involved. Although it's been demonized by christianity, brujería represents a rich tapestry of cultural and spiritual traditions that continue to evolve and adapt within the diverse cultural landscape of Mexico and beyond.

Nahum asked his benefactors if they would loan him a few items and take him out into the night so he could perform a contact ritual. Knowing this was the last night of his visit, they agreed. Nahum said he needed to borrow some alcohol and alter candles—two of each: Saint Brigid, Saint Guadalupe, and St. Jude. Saint Brigid is known for her piety, generosity, and kindness.

Our Lady of Guadalupe is the honored title of the Virgin Mary, is considered the patroness of Mexico, and is revered by millions of Catholics throughout the Americas. Saint Jude is one of the apostles of Jesus, traditionally known as the patron saint of desperate and impossible causes, illness, or despair. These candles are often used in Catholic liturgical practices, including during the celebration of mass and the veneration of saints. Altar candles are integral to the catholic liturgy, symbolizing Christ as the Light of the World.

However, in brujeria, the meanings have often been adapted or altered over time. These candles' representation and meaning to Nahum and his bruja were unknown. He said he needed to be taken to a place between dirt and concrete, and while driving, Nahum pointed to a bridge, which he felt would facilitate the ritual appropriately. Climbing out of the backseat, he took his materials.

"You need to drive off of the bridge and face away. Do not look back. I will come to the car when I am done." He studied the two. Marcos nodded. "You must not look back," he ordered severely.

Teresa and Marcos pulled away from the bridge and parked. In the rearview mirror, the couple caught glimpses of sparks as Nahum lit the candles and arranged them in a star around him. He poured alcohol into some esoteric pattern and then took a swig. Holding the sixth candle in his hands as he sat at the center of the formation, he began to command an unseen spirit.

The couple made a valiant effort not to look but grew increasingly curious as they heard him chanting and performing a fascinating ancient ceremony.

"He said not to look," the wife reminded her husband.

"I wasn't." he insisted. They began to make small talk to distract each other when Teresa saw Marcos adjust the rearview mirror to better spy.

"Hey! You're peeking. I can tell!" She chided but stopped talking short when she noticed he was holding his breath. She peered at him inquisitively, seeing beads of sweat nervously forming on his temple and upper lip. Turning around, she looked back to see Nahum chanting reverentially, arms raised powerfully. A dim light seemed to be illuminating him under the twinkling stars. She squinted through the dark, double-checking her vision in disbelief as he lifted his arms higher; the candles rose from the pavement, levitating above, encircling him. The candle in his hand flickered as it rose, forming a pinnacle on the pentagram. A circular current lifted all of the leaves surrounding him into a whirlwind. It culminated by toppling back down as he bowed his head and lowered his voice, concluding his séance as the candles floated back to the ground in perfect formation.

At this, Teresa began to pray, and Marcos turned on the ignition. He sped away in a panic, fearful that the forces that young Nahum called upon were sinister. Teresa held her breath until they were a block away.

"That was scary," she said, hand on her chest. As she uttered the words, Marcos slammed on the brakes, knocking the breath out of her. She looked up to see Nahum standing right in front of the hood. He banged on the hood three times forcefully.

"Hello, there. Come on in," Marcos said helplessly. Teresa nervously squeezed her husband's bicep as the boy opened the back door and climbed into the back seat. Eyes narrowed into slits; he sat down in the seat, seeming more wild beast than a man. The couple drove back home. Nahum walked inside their house and into the bedroom where he'd been staying. They locked their bedroom door and barely slept a wink that night. They stayed in their room until it was time to drive Nahum back to the train station. To their surprise, he was already gone.

Twenty years later, Teresa was running an errand in town, and as she passed by the train station, she saw him. Frightened, she took a closer look. It was him, she determined. Strangely, he still looked the same, barely out of his teens. He was wearing the same clothes, dirty and ragged, and when he looked up at her, he had a wildly sinister look in his eye. She broke eye contact and drove on. Fortunately, she never saw him again, although she wonders sometimes about timid Nahum from Vera Cruz and his bruja.

Saved by the Boy

As time passed, Teresa became a mother to a three-year-old son, Devon. He was a good little boy, and she enjoyed spending time with him. There was a night when they were on the couch watching television when she fell asleep. She began to dream a peculiar dream. Perplexed, she looked around and saw that she was floating around in the house. From her bedroom, she could hear the TV playing downstairs. Interested to learn who was downstairs in this dream, she floated down the staircase and could see herself and her little boy. Devon was fixated on the show while she lay unconscious.

Cuddling into his mother, Devon noticed his mother was cold and lying unnaturally still. Instinctively frightened, he shook her to wake her even though he was only a toddler. She didn't stir. Her hand fell away from her body, and her head lolled back lifelessly.

'Mommy!" Devon began to cry, slapping her arm. She could feel her body becoming lighter, warmer, and more buoyant, increasingly detached from the scene unfolding before her. She floated up higher into the ceiling and almost out of the house. She forced herself to tune back into the scenario below.

"Mama," Devon screamed, hot tears streaking his face. He was standing on the floor, yanking her hand so hard he began to pull her body off the couch, but she didn't show any signs of life. "Come back, Mommy,"

Devon pleaded. This got her attention, and using all her strength, she pulled herself back down to where her son stood, wailing next to his mother's body, which seemed devoid of spirit. She felt obliged to comfort him, but he could not see her here in this form. "No, Mommy. Come back," he sobbed, choking on his tears.

At this appeal, she began to swim against the current, strife, and hardship of life in this human body and get back to her son. She decided to return.

Once she had made that choice, she coughed and sputtered, trying to sit up. She felt as if her neck had been twisted in an abnormal position and was sore. Her throat was so dry she could only croak for water, which Devon picked up off the coffee table and handed her. She drank the entire glass before she got a full gasping breath as if she'd gone hours without air. Teresa panted and coughed, holding her son close to her heart as he wept tears of joy. More tired than she'd ever been and incredibly thirsty, she drank two more glasses of water. Tucking Devon in for the night, she crawled to bed. She slept deeply that night and into the next afternoon before waking with only the bizarre memory of an unexplained out-of-body experience.

Μαριτα Χηριστινε Λορβιεχκε

Phantom of the Tribal Monastery

In the heart of Santa Fe Tribal Lands, six-year-old Hank's childhood unfolded against a spiritual backdrop. In this close-knit native community, the boundaries between the living and the spirits of the departed often blurred, and the tales of the supernatural wove themselves into everyday life. Near their home, a crumbling, long-abandoned monastery stood as a solemn reminder of times long past.

Once, it had been a catholic school, but years of neglect had taken their toll. In its final days, a few aging nuns had called it home, living out their final years in seclusion and depravity until death. Hank's father, a law enforcement officer, bore the duty of keeping an eye on the decaying structure, a hazard to the public and a haven for vagrants seeking refuge, often leaving behind destruction in their wake.

One evening, Hank accompanied his father to leave a note for any intruders, asking them to vacate the premises come morning. While there, Hank's father, ever the compassionate soul, encountered a homeless man who had sought refuge within the crumbling walls. His father informed the man of the dangers and advised him to move on as soon as possible.

Meanwhile, Hank, curiosity brimming, wandered away from the adults, exploring the debris-strewn interior. He glimpsed something: the towering figure of a man lurking in the shadows, a massive, looming presence watching them. Hank's gaze locked on him, eyes filled with apprehension.

The formidable man approached him, moving with determination, freezing Hank in his tracks. Panic welled as the stranger broke into a run, closing the distance between them. Just as it seemed the stranger would collide with the terrified boy, he vanished into thin air, leaving behind only a chilling, spectral emptiness.

Hank's fear erupted. He began to cry, trembling and frightened. He realized then that he had encountered something far beyond the realm of the living, a ghost, a restless spirit from another plane. Rushing to his father, he recounted the event. To his dismay, the two men had seen or heard nothing out of the ordinary. As they stood, father and son, they spoke of the building's dark history, the countless lives that had met their end within its forsaken walls over the years. It was not implausible, they mused, that the spirits of those who had suffered and perished there still lingered, their unrest etching an indelible mark on the decaying building and the grounds that surrounded it. The shadows of the monastery held secrets that the living might never fully fathom.

Numen of the Night

Hank's family had eventually left northern New Mexico and settled in Roswell, where he transitioned into young adulthood, encountering four episodes of sleep paralysis over three years. One particularly unsettling incident unfolded just after his high school graduation, shrouding his night in terror.

At the unearthly hour of 3 am, Hank woke, parched throat compelling him to seek refuge in a refreshing gulp of water. With sleepy determination, he emerged from his bed, going through the dimly lit house towards the kitchen, water beckoning. Walking back from the fridge, Hank guzzled the bottle's contents as he returned to bed.

A solitary illumination source flickered faintly in his room, an intimate night bulb heat lamp casting a subtle glow, thanks to the enclosure of his pet snake. Oblivious to the impending strangeness, Hank deposited the empty bottle on the floor beside his bed. Weary and ready to return to the embrace of slumber, he settled face-first onto the pillow. Just as he was about to surrender to the soothing pull of sleep, the world around him took on a disquieting transformation.

Across from the enclosure housing his python, a shadow began to unfurl across the wall. It was a shadow with substance, as though an unseen presence had materialized before his eyes. The reflexive urge to turn his head towards this apparition tugged at Hank, but to his growing horror, his body remained paralyzed, a silent captive of his nocturnal ordeal.

Amidst this surreal tableau, a haunting sound emerged a peculiar auditory experience that Hank could only liken to a plastic static. It was not an ethereal electric hum but a tangible aural intrusion, as if many people in a cavernous stadium were collectively fidgeting with crinkling butterscotch wrappers. This disconcerting symphony of noise swelled gradually within his ears, intensifying his distress with every passing second.

Fighting against the invisible restraints that held him in place, Hank struggled to break free from the oppressive grip of sleep paralysis. His curiosity was overtaken by fear as he agonized over who or what could lurk behind him, obscuring the enclosure of his reptile. The entity seemed to inch closer, step by unseen step, until it reached his bed's foot.

Then, with an unsettling transition, it floated horizontally over him, casting an ominous shadow that enveloped him in a chilling embrace. Despite his futile attempts to escape the paralyzing grip of his own body, Hank remained immobilized, a powerless spectator to the bizarre event unfolding before him.

Finally, the entity uttered a faint, hair-raising sound, a scream that seemed to resonate beyond the boundaries of ordinary perception. It was as if Hank heard a dog whistle, a sound perceptible only in its subtle vibrations yet profoundly impacting the very fabric of his surroundings. This disconcerting auditory phenomenon persisted for several agonizing seconds before gradually fading away.

As the entity withdrew, it didn't exit the room but retreated into the darkness. Only when Hank's paralyzed state released its grip did he manage to turn around, his heart threatening to burst out of his chest. In the end, he was left alone in the empty stillness of his room. A disturbing feeling gnawing at him as he contemplated the horrendous nature of the experience. The empty bottle of water, sitting right where he had placed it before the episode, confirmed that the incident was not a dream but an account that defied any logical explanation.

The second event unfolded a year after the initial encounter. Hank found himself at his ex-girlfriend's house, which he was familiar with, though it had an unnerving vibe when the family was away. It was around 3:30 in the morning when she woke him, needing a ride to work. Upon returning to the silent house, he amused himself idly on his phone. The clock indicated the late hour encouraged him to get some sleep. His phone, fully charged and plugged in, sat beside him as he lay there, listening to the hushed sounds of the night.

However, this night was destined to be different. Hank experienced another episode, one that started with an auditory anomaly. It was as though someone had taken a dial to the volume of the world around him, slowly reducing the cacophony to a deathly silence. This aberrant experience left him puzzled, especially when he tried to move. To his surprise, his eyes were wide open, staring at the bedroom wall. He noticed his phone resting beside his head, a comforting presence in the obscurity.

Then, the strange phenomenon struck again, and the plastic-static noise from the previous encounter began. The initial seconds were marked by confusion as the memory of the last episode resurfaced, replaced swiftly by fear. Hank struggled to move, to break free from the immobilizing grip of whatever unknown force was at play. His senses then detected unusual activity in the kitchen, dishes clattering, pots, and pans being moved around. Something unseen darted from the kitchen into his room, stopping abruptly at the foot of his bed.

The inhuman thrumming scream echoed through the room once more, low and unsettling as if it had a palpable effect on the surroundings. The wicked presence lingered at the foot of the bed. Its motives were unfathomable. It retreated after about 30 nerve-wracking seconds, and Hank finally regained control of his body. His immediate instinct was to reach for his phone, only to discover that the few minutes he had spent in this nightmarish scenario had drained the device almost completely. Shaken but determined, Hank left the room, walking through the undisturbed kitchen. The dogs, usually sensitive to disturbances, remained unfazed, their behavior unchanged.

    The third incident occurred in the summer of 2020. Hank had traveled to Lubbock, Texas, to retrieve some forgotten items for his apartment in Roswell. As night fell, he settled down as usual, attempting to find rest. Once more, the plastic-static noise returned, signaling the onset of another hellish event. This time, Hank could hear the door to his room creak open, and a fiendish presence moved slowly closer to his bed. The breathing of this entity, laden with irritation, reached his ears, devoid of any muffling. Despite the escalating tension, Hank's curiosity began to outweigh his fear.

He struggled desperately to turn and face whatever lurked behind him but became immobilized again. The encounter was brief this time. The presence entered the room, exuding anger, and left without a sound. As it exited, the door closed behind it, and Hank's mobility returned instantly. Surprisingly, he felt less afraid this time, his determination unwavering. He sprang from the bed and scrutinized every corner of his apartment, yet found no trace of the mysterious intruder.

The fourth and most recent incident occurred approximately six to eight months after the third. Hank had recounted all his bizarre experiences to his mother's boyfriend, sharing his desire to confront whatever haunted him. The older man offered a cryptic warning, advising Hank to be cautious about his wishes. The very next morning, around 6 am, as Hank lay in his grandparents' house, an upsetting sensation jolted him awake. Something was tapping his foot rhythmically, persistently. He tried to turn to identify the source of the disturbance but found himself trapped in a state of paralysis, the familiar plastic-static noise reverberating in his ears. Then, the entity began to tug at the sheets.

The taps continued relentlessly, a message that seemed to taunt him. It felt as though the furtive presence was goading him to confront it, to face the source of his torment. But Hank, firmly guided by an instinct for self-preservation, chose not to yield to the provocation. He remained steadfast in his refusal to turn and acknowledge the enigma that had haunted his nights for so long.

Phantom that Followed

JD, the son of Josie and John Lorbiecke, had accepted a new job out of state back in January 2020. As the time approached for him to leave, he informed his friends, and they individually visited him to bid farewell and wish him a safe journey. One evening, their family friend Hank came to visit. On such occasions, JD's wife, Marita, would prepare an epic meal, and they gathered around the dinner table to chat the night. As the evening progressed, the conversation took a spooky turn. "I had the strangest experience last night," Hank shared with JD. "I was lying on my side, dead asleep, and suddenly I woke up but couldn't move. I was in a state of sleep paralysis."

Curious, JD inquired, "What do you think woke you up?" Hank explained that he had been awakened by a devilish force pulling on his bedsheets. Whatever was pulling the sheet was behind him, and he had been lying on his left side, facing the wall. The unknown entity kept tugging at the blankets near his shoulders. Despite being unable to move, the sheets were not pulled off him, even though the tugging continued for several minutes.

Suddenly, the paralysis lifted, and Hank swiftly rolled over to see who or what had disturbed him, only to find no one there.

"It scared the hell out of me," Hank admitted. "I've had sleep paralysis episodes since I was a little kid, but it hadn't happened in a long time. So, it caught me by surprise."

JD reassured him, saying, "It was probably just a strangely vivid dream. Nothing was bothering you last night. You must have been sleeping deeply." As the evening continued, they enjoyed their dinner and talked late into the night, discussing dreams, the future, and more. Eventually, Hank bid his farewell, and it was time for JD to embark on his journey to his new job. After kissing his beloved wife goodbye, he hit the road. This drive marked the beginning of a transition filled with anxious excitement.

Just after sunset, he barreled east on a seldom-traveled road. Within 20 minutes, darkness swallowed the landscape, with only his headlights and occasional passing semi-trucks breaking the obsidian veil. He listened to a podcast featuring stories about serial killers and ghostly encounters, passing the time.

Startled. He glimpsed something in his peripheral vision in the passenger seat. He turned his head. He blinked, peering into the dark. Nothing was there except shadows cast by the passing trucks.

Blinding lights and a blaring horn of an oncoming semi bellowed JD's drift into oncoming traffic. With a jerk of the wheel, he corrected and returned his focus to the road, white-knuckling the steering wheel.

Bristled, the driver chose to find some upbeat music in hopes of easing his nerves. The remainder of the drive was uneventful, and he safely reached his destination, thankful for the safe arrival. However, a lingering sense of discord remained. Upon arriving at his temporary lodging, JD unloaded his car and settled in. As he went about his tasks, he couldn't shake the feeling that he was not alone. Yet again, he saw a shadowy figure in the passenger seat but chose not to examine it further. Instead, he focused on his preparations for the night.

After watching TV, JD tossed the blankets back and crawled into bed. Sleep eluded him. An early morning awaited him, and he hoped for a few hours of rest before his busy day began. He lay on his back, staring at the ceiling. He couldn't help but recall the strange occurrences of the evening. Eventually, he rolled over onto his left side, facing the door.

At 4:00 am, blinked, perceiving the inky darkness of the unfamiliar room. He felt a gentle tug on his shoulder as if someone were trying to wake him. Another tug followed. Now, he was wide awake but found himself unable to move. Eyes open, the room remained masked in obscurity.

As he lay immobilized, a sensation of dread threatened to drown him. One tug and another in quick succession. Fully alert. The paralysis overpowered him. He prayed silently, reciting the Lord's Prayer in his mind. With the utterance of the final words, the paralysis lifted.

Freed from its grip, he sat up on the edge of the bed and listened intently. The room was silent. After a moment, he got up, turned on the bathroom light, and searched every nook and cranny of the room, even checking under the bed and inside the closets. He found no intruder. He was in a locked, empty room.

Satisfied that he was alone, he said the prayer aloud, turned off the light and drifted into a dreamless slumber. In the following weeks, JD visited home and learned that Hank had slept peacefully since their last conversation. Hank thanked JD for taking that monkey off his back. JD attributed his relief from the spirit to the power of prayer.

Journey Beyond

Sue Mosbrucker, a compassionate soul and sister to John Lorbiecke, had dedicated her life to the noble cause of hospice care. She had walked alongside those on the fragile precipice of existence for years, offering comfort, solace, and unwavering support. Hospice care was her calling, a sacred mission to ease the journey of those facing the twilight of their lives.

Sue knew every patient's story was unique, yet they all converged at the same destination: the end of life's winding path. Her role was to enhance the quality of their final chapters and bring comfort, dignity, and emotional solace to the patients and their families, who clung to precious moments.

Sue worked within the patient's home, where familiarity and cherished memories surrounded them. She knew that the heart of hospice care lay in the bonds formed with the patients and their caretakers. She was the bridge between this world and the next, a lifeline for those who had no one else.

In her years of service, Sue had witnessed the profound transformations that marked her clients' final days and moments. As they drew closer to the threshold between life and the great unknown, subtle changes occurred. Each shift was as unique as the individual, shaped by their beliefs, experiences, and physical condition.

In these sacred moments, common threads wove through the tapestry. Patients often withdrew from the hustle and bustle of the world, finding solace in solitude or the comforting presence of cherished family and friends. Those who found themselves alone took additional comfort in Sue. Energy waned as the body succumbed to the relentless march of time, yielding to the ravages of illness.

Consciousness itself was in flux, a delicate dance between realms. Some entered states of confusion, experiencing moments of disorientation as their perceptions shifted. Medications and the natural progression of dying played their parts, painting a unique portrait for each traveler. Appetite and thirst waned as the body's systems gradually surrendered to the inevitable. Sleep and drowsiness overtook them, a gentle retreat into the comforting embrace of slumber, a response to the body's dwindling energy reserves. Pain and discomfort became perpetual companions in their last days, and Sue worked tirelessly to ensure that each patient found solace in the sunset of their life.

What struck Sue most profoundly were the ethereal experiences that transcended the physical world. Visions and encounters with those beyond the mortal world manifest. Patients saw loved ones long departed, feeling a sense of peace and transcendence that defied explanation. Amidst these poignant moments, Sue bore witness to interactions that surpassed the confines of the living, conversing with those who'd crossed over, reaching out guided by a loving hand. These encounters often culminated in a peaceful passing, a conversion into the next existence, leaving Sue in awe of the profound mysteries of life's final journey.

She came to accept what had once bewildered her with grace and reverence. Sue understood that in the sacred space where one's earthly journey met its end, the veil between worlds grew thin, and glimpses into the realms beyond became possible. As she continued her work, Sue carried the profound wisdom that life's ultimate passage was a miraculous and mysterious journey beyond comprehension, a trip into the infinite unknown.

Heart of Darkness

In a quiet, remote neighborhood in Blackfoot, Idaho, the youngest brother of Josie, JD, found himself alone, immersed in the task of fixing the water supply at a fixer-upper that he and his wife Lori. Not unlike his sister, JD was sensitive to spiritual activity. He was unsettled as the air hung heavily with a sense of foreboding, and the house seemed to exude an unsettling aura. With tools in hand, he entered, the door creaking open as he stepped over the threshold. In case of need for a speedy exit, he left the door ajar, a lifeline to the outside world.

JD's work inside was tedious, water pipes echoing through the empty rooms. With relief, he finally completed his task and ventured outside to turn the water supply on and off, a routine step in the repair process. The sun hung low on the horizon, casting long shadows that danced across the overgrown yard. As he stood in the fading light, a chill setting in, he completed his work and headed back towards the open door. His breath quickened as he realized something was amiss. The door, which he had left ajar, was now firmly shut and locked as if it had been closed by an invisible hand. Panic gripped him, knowing he was not alone as he jiggled the doorknob. It refused to yield.

His heart thumping, he frantically pounded on the door, but the silence of the desolate house seemed to swallow his cries. The darkness of the interior loomed before him. An icy chill slithered down his spine. JD fumbled for his phone with trembling hands, desperate to call for assistance, but the battery was drained, leaving him alone. Shadows danced on the walls, and the house groaned in response to his fear.

His gloves were wet and freezing. He only had a windbreaker on despite the onset of winter. Locked out and trapped in the fading light, JD could feel the presence of something vile. A nefarious force coupled with the frozen night taunted him. The last rays of daylight disappeared. He was left with a sinking realization, though the only person on site, he was not alone. The locked door slammed shut, truck keys inside, phone dead, chill setting in, maliciously trapping him in the heart of darkness. After hours of attempting to jimmy the windows with the few tools he had on hand, he walked around looking for a brick to break a window and damage his newly purchased property. When we walked back around front, we saw the door open with his car keys sitting on the threshold. He wasted no time driving home and telling Lori about his afternoon while he warmed his belly with a hot meal.

Peeping Poltergeist

In 2015, Josie found herself at Providence St. Patrick Hospital in Missoula, Montana, where the stark, sterile corridors seemed to echo with the whispers of countless souls seeking solace. She had come for a routine CT scan, the promise of answers and uncertainty hanging heavily in the air. A kind nurse greeted her with a crisp white gown, instructing her to divest herself of all jewelry before the procedure. With trepidation, Josie placed her belongings into the small bag provided. She watched it disappear into a secure locker, locking away a piece of her identity.

The examination itself was an exercise in stillness. Josie lay on the cold, stainless steel table, barely daring to breathe as the machine worked its technological magic. The minutes felt like hours. She released a long-held breath when the tech came over the loudspeaker, informing her the exam was over. A reassuring presence in the clinic, the nurse returned with her belongings in a sack, instructing her to call out when dressed. Josie entered the changing area, where a long, heavy curtain hung, offering a semblance of privacy. She removed the gown and began dressing.

Focused on the task, a sudden chill coursed through the room. She shivered. Drawn securely, the curtain began to move of its own accord, slowly inching back to reveal the hospital corridor.

Her heart quickened as she called out, "I'm not yet dressed," holding her blouse closed. Josie approached the curtain with a determined stride, yanking it closed with trembling hands. She peeked out. Her eyes darted across the room, seeking an explanation. The nurse was diligently working at her station at the end of the hall, her attention absorbed by the reports on her monitor. No one else was in sight, and there was no rational explanation for the curtain's movement.

Hastily, Josie donned the rest of her clothing, disquiet growing with every passing second. The curtain waved in the center as if someone was toying with her, her body in full view. The room seemed to inhabit the phantom of a disembodied peeping tom. As she left the room, she couldn't shake the feeling that the hospital corridors concealed secrets beyond the realm of the living, and the creepy encounter would linger in her memory long after she had left its sterile embrace.

Love Beyond the Veil

In the sweltering summer of 2023, Ernest Aguayo, brother of Josie, found himself in the depths of grief, haunted by the recent loss of his beloved girlfriend, Rosa Marie Pena, who had succumbed to a devastating stroke. The weight of sorrow pressed upon him, and the world seemed a shadowy, lonely place without Rosa's light.

One night, as the oppressive heat clung to the walls of his home, Ernie sat alone on the couch, the room bathed in the soft glow of the television. The air was thick with memories and emptiness that lingers after loss. In the night's quiet, he saw a shadowy figure, unmistakably Rosa, standing in the corner of the room. His heart skipped a beat as he watched her ethereal form, her presence a bittersweet reminder of their love.

With longing and disbelief, he witnessed Rosa walking through the kitchen wall, disappearing into the hallway beyond. He smiled, knowing that although the love of his life had passed on, he was not alone.

A separate encounter came when Ernie found himself face-to-face with the phantom of his grandmother, Guelita, as she was affectionately known. She stood at the sink as if washing dishes, but the kitchen was inexplicably pristine, devoid of dirty dishes or clutter.
Confusion and curiosity welled up within Ernie as he questioned the apparition. "What are you doing?" In response, the ghostly figure turned toward him, her eyes filled with a loving warmth that exceeded the boundaries between living and dead. She smiled, and a gesture of profound affection washed over Ernie, leaving him with a sense of peace he had never known.

And then, on yet another night, the boundaries between the realms of the living and the deceased blurred once more. Still grappling with grief, Ernie saw a figure in the doorway, a silhouette that strongly resembled his dear friend Rosa's cousin Jamie, who had spent much time with him and her cousin.

Her presence, though ghostly, radiated a sense of comfort and reassurance as if to convey that love and friendship endure even beyond the confines of mortality.

In those haunted moments, the barricade between the worlds grew thin, allowing Ernie to glimpse the spectral echoes of their loved ones. The encounters served as a touching reminder that the bonds of love are eternal, and the departed can find ways to reach out from the other side, offering solace and a glimpse into the mysteries that lie beyond.

Shade of The Shining

Ian, a friend of Dimitris Rentzios, son of Mary Ann, had personally hunted Europe and heard with his ears the Phantoms of the Battle of the Bulge and the 1779 Battle of Bull's Inlet in South Carolina. After chasing a Patriot merchant ship aground, a British privateer tried to board it. After a hard fight, the British won the vessel. The remnants of this bloody event have echoed throughout time.

The Battle of the Bulge, which occurred during World War II from December 16, 1944, to January 25, 1945, was one of the largest and bloodiest battles fought on the Western Front. The battle occurred in the densely forested Ardennes region of Belgium, Luxembourg, and France and involved intense combat between American, British, and German forces. While there are no specific legends or widespread claims of supernatural phenomena associated with the Battle of the Bulge comparable to other famous wartime ghost stories, the battle itself was marked by the haunting experiences of soldiers who endured extreme conditions and witnessed the horrors of war.

These experiences, combined with the natural darkness of the Ardennes forests, have contributed to a sense of haunting in the region.

Some soldiers who fought in the Battle of the Bulge reported dread in the thick forests, especially during the bitterly cold and foggy winter days and nights. The dense fog and the sounds of combat created an atmosphere that could easily play tricks on the imagination. Exhausted soldiers might have mistaken sounds or shadows for something ghostly amid their stress and fatigue. It's essential to recognize the immense human suffering, sacrifice, and trauma during this historic battle, which has left a lasting impact on the collective memory of those who lived through it and those who study it today.

In the heart of a moonless night, Ian and his comrades huddled together around a campfire on a long-forgotten battlefield, where the scars of war still whispered their harrowing tales to those willing to listen. The fire crackled softly, its warm glow the only respite from the enveloping darkness that clung to the desolate landscape.

As the men shared quiet conversations and sipped on steaming mugs of bitter coffee, the campfire provided a sedate backdrop, gently popping a familiar lullaby in this bleak, ghostly realm. The stars above offered a feeble glimmer of hope in the void of night, and for a fleeting moment, it seemed the world had found a fragile sense of peace.

But then, as if summoned by the tortured reverberations of the past, the tranquility shattered. The air grew thick with tension as the night unleashed horrors upon them. From all angles, the cacophony of battle erupted like a vengeful symphony: shouts of fear, the deafening roar of artillery, and the anguished cries of men caught in the throes of violence. The men were overwhelmed, their senses assaulted by this sudden onslaught. Once a beacon of comfort, the campfire flickered and dimmed in the face of the encroaching darkness. Fear clutched at their hearts as they scrambled for weapons, their faces engraved with primal terror.

But as swiftly as it had begun, the nightmarish crescendo of battle faded into melancholy silence. The battlefield, which had come alive with the tortured resonances of its past, returned to its funereal stillness. The men were left shaken and disoriented, their minds struggling to reconcile the tranquility of the campfire with the violent phantoms that had besieged them. At that moment, they knew restless memories surrounded them. The ghosts of war had risen from the depths of history to remind them that even in the quietest moments, the horrors of the past could claw their way back to the surface, leaving them forever haunted by the shadows of battle.

In 2003, Dimitris Rentzios, the son of Mary Ann, went on a quest to have some ghostly encounters and book a night's stay at the famous Stanley Hotel. This renowned inn is located in Estes Park, Colorado, and is a historic and famously haunted hotel that inspired Stephen King's novel, "The Shining." The third floor of the Stanley Hotel is said to be one of the most haunted areas in the building. Guests and staff have reported various paranormal experiences on this floor.

Some of the reported paranormal activity on the third floor of the Stanley Hotel includes ghostly apparitions. Guests have claimed to see shadowy figures and apparitions wandering the halls. Phantom sounds, including mysterious footsteps, voices, and laughter, have been heard when no one else is around. Flickering lights and electronic devices are known to malfunction or turn on and off. Guests have experienced unexplained cold spots and drops in temperature on the third floor. Some visitors have reported objects mysteriously moving or being rearranged in their rooms.

The Stanley Hotel embraces its haunted reputation and even offers ghost tours and paranormal-themed events for guests interested in exploring its supernatural history. Whether you're a believer in the paranormal or simply curious, a visit to the third floor of the Stanley Hotel can be an intriguing experience.

"The Shining" is a classic horror novel written by Stephen King and later adapted into a famous film directed by Stanley Kubrick. The story has a profoundly spooky premise:

Jack Torrance, a struggling writer and recovering alcoholic, accepts a job as the winter caretaker of the historic Overlook Hotel, nestled in the Colorado Rockies. The hotel, isolated and cut off from the outside world during the harsh winter months, needs someone to maintain it during this period. Jack sees it as an opportunity to work on his writing and reconnect with his wife, Wendy, and their young son, Danny. As the Torrance family settles into their new home, they are unaware of the hotel's dark history and supernatural presence. However, it becomes clear that the Overlook Hotel is no ordinary place. The isolation and the evil forces within the hotel take a toll on Jack's sanity. Meanwhile, Danny, who possesses a psychic ability known as "the shining," begins to experience disturbing visions of the hotel's past and its violent events.

The hotel's dark influence intensifies, and Jack's descent into madness becomes more pronounced. His violent and erratic behavior, especially young Danny, puts his family in grave danger. He becomes a target of the supernatural entities that haunt the Overlook, the hotel's name in the book and film.

The spooky premise of "The Shining" revolves around the psychological horror of isolation, the disintegration of a family, and the malevolent forces lurking within the hotel's haunted walls. It explores themes of addiction, madness, and the intersection of the supernatural with the human psyche. The story's tension and terror build as the family becomes trapped in the hotel, struggling to survive the growing horror both from within and outside themselves.

This story fascinated Dimitris and his ghost-hunting buddy Ian, a paranormal veteran. Ian was back in the States, and in league with Dimitris in the unforgiving winter of 2004, the adventurers embarked on a chilling adventure, braving the frozen embrace of Estes Park, Colorado, to spend a night in the notorious Stanley Hotel. Their choice of lodging was none other than the very room where the master of horror himself, Stephen King, had stayed during the filming of "The Shining." The hotel had become the stuff of legends, known far and wide for its spectral inhabitants and the tales that clung to its historic walls.

They checked into their room. The oppressive cold of the Colorado winter pressed against the windows. The room was small, with only a bed and restroom, starkly contrasting the vast, ice-covered landscape that stretched beyond the hotel's walls.

Not particularly adventurous regarding culinary choices, Ian had decided to indulge in a milkshake earlier in the day, unaware of the lactic revenge it would reap on his intestines. Meanwhile, Dimitris, thankful for his digestive resilience, amusedly shook his head at his friend's predicament.

Dimitris searched for the audio recorder they had brought along for their expedition. A series of loud bangs rang from the restroom where Ian sought refuge. "Buddy!" Dimitris called out, chuckling. "I told you not to have that Blizzard after lunch."

Ian's voice, muffled by the bathroom door, came with a note of genuine distress.

"Not funny! Quit banging on the door. I'm dying in here." Dimitris sobered. The hair raised on his arms as he replied,

"Dude, that wasn't me." Confusion and trepidation filled the room as Ian, now anxious and uncomfortable, pleaded with Dimitris to stop the unnerving prank. But Dimitris knew that something supernatural was unfolding before them.

Once they rested and Ian recovered from releasing the Kraken into the Outlook's commode, they decided to venture out into the wintry night, their digital audio recorder in use. Ian tucked the recorder under the bench outside their door to capture any happenings in the hall while they were away. The tales of the hotel's paranormal history filled their thoughts as they explored the surrounding grounds, including a nearby cemetery and pet cemetery that seemed energized with aberrant energy. Each step they took through the deep, dark forest was punctuated by the powdery crunch of snow beneath their boots.

The night was ominously silent. The world around them frozen. Their breath hung in the air like gossamer specters. Despite the cold, they pressed on, snapping photographs, hoping to film glimpses of the other side.

As the clock neared three am, exhaustion overtook them. They returned to the hotel's warmly lit foyer. To their surprise, the sound of a piano being cheerily played reached their ears, even though the hour was late, and the hotel was abandoned except for a skeletal crew.

Approaching the piano, they were taken aback to find the piano seat empty. The tinkling of classical music filled the vestibule with an evocative melody.

Dimitris, leaning closer to inspect the piano, watched in fascination as the music ceased, the final notes fading. Ian, eager to engage, remarked to the hotel staff. "That's cool. How does it work?" The clerk, engrossed in her paperwork, hardly looked up.
"How? I guess when this ghost gets bored, he plays us a tune. I'm sick of it, to be honest." Looking up, she grimaced.

The revelation left the two friends astonished. The piano's ghostly serenades were a nightly occurrence, a fact that the faculty had grown accustomed to. Filled with excitement, Dimitris and Ian hurriedly retrieved their audio recorder and returned to the lobby, hoping to capture the pianist in action. They sat in anticipation for almost an hour, but the apparition had moved on, eluding their efforts.

Disappointed but invigorated by their authentic encounter, they retired for a few hours of sleep. Checking out the following day, they were satisfied. Their adventure at the historic Stanley Hotel was a success.

Returning home, Ian connected the audio recorder to his computer and listened to the recordings. Betwixt the crackling and static, their voices were clear, but another presence joined the audio at midnight. The faint sound of tiny footsteps padded through the hallway, followed by the compelling voice of a young girl singing a melancholic tune. The poltergeist paced back and forth in eternal restlessness, her vaporous figure unseen but undeniably present.

As Ian and Dimitris played the recording repeatedly, their amazement grew. They had captured evidence of one of the hotel's phantoms. The tape became a keepsake of their unforgettable adventure at the Stanley Hotel, a testament to the epic adventures within its historic walls.

Shadows

Emmie, daughter of Marita and JD Lorbiecke, age 12, whispered her suspicions to her best friend, Azilynn, during a sleepover at her house. The room was cloaked in a hush, with only the faint glow of the nightlight piercing the shadows. She confessed that, at times, an unshakable feeling of not being alone would wash over her, or she'd catch elusive glimpses of something inexplicable darting just beyond her vision. Azilynn's excitement surged like an electric current through the room, pulse racing in suspense.

Eager to provoke the presence, she ventured out into the dimly lit hallway, her voice carrying a brazen tone as she taunted, "Hey, Ghost. Come out!"

Emmie, a note of caution in her voice, hurried after her friend, urging restraint and explaining that the entity had always seemed benign, never causing harm. They wandered up and down the hall, curiosity mingling with trepidation. Losing interest, Azilynn strolled into the living room and plopped down onto the couch with the remote having moved on. Emmie's heart skipped a beat as her gaze passed by a dark figure, hauntingly similar in size to hers, manifesting near the closet. The room seemed to hold its breath as the specter suspended in the air.

Emmie, choosing to maintain her model of ignorance, feigned oblivion of the apparition, and when it didn't seem to get any attention, it flickered momentarily and, like a wisp of smoke, faded into obscurity. Emmie, relaxing, joined Azilynn on the couch, putting her feet into her friend's lap. Azilynn begged for popcorn as she announced they would be watching Twilight: New Moon. Emmie was delighted by the distracted bustling about the kitchen preparing snacks.

Once charged with suspense, the room bore witness to their silent resolve to neither provoke nor encourage the enigmatic force that coexisted with them in the shadows.

Holiday Spirit

A few years later, Emmie, 14 years old, was immersed in the kitchen's heart on a crisp, snowy evening, the soft glow of twinkling holiday lights casting a warm and cozy ambiance. The comforting scent of home-cooked delights wafted through the air, teasing her senses as her mother worked her culinary magic. Her mother was boiling cacao to make her famous Mayan Hot Cocoa. On the other burners, fluffy tortilla dough was browning on the *comal* while the green chili stew aromatically simmered and steamed. Anton, her younger brother, was dutifully washing dishes at the sink, his hands immersed in the warm, soapy water. At the same time, a holiday playlist softly serenaded them with familiar tunes of merriment. The kitchen was adorned with festive decorations, from garlands of evergreen boughs to a sparkling Christmas tree decorated with ornaments that held cherished memories.

Emmie was delightedly engrossed in her project, crafting a gingerbread house with nimble fingers, each sweet, sugary wall a work of confectionery art. Her indulgent side couldn't resist, and she intermittently nibbled from the dessert tray, savoring the sugary decadence that danced upon her taste buds.

As she sat at the bar, her gaze absentmindedly fixated on the opposite side of the kitchen, a shiver of excitement coursed through her. The room was alive with the spirit of the holiday. The magical atmosphere seemed to infuse every corner. The joyful laughter of family accompanied the once-familiar sounds of culinary orchestration gathered in the cozy room. The kitchen window was steamed from the wonders boiling on the cook stove.

Then, as if summoned by the enchantment of the holiday, the kitchen floor near the fridge released a spine-tingling creak—a sound that, at this moment, felt like a playful, mischievous guest joining the festivities. Emmie's fingers froze mid-nibble, and she felt her heart quicken, not in fear but in the embrace of the holiday wonder.

She exchanged wide-eyed glances of bewilderment with Anton, both sharing an unspoken sense that something extraordinary was unfolding before them. The snow continued to fall gently outside. They cherished the season's enchantment, leaving the unusual, real or imagined, to become another cherished tale to recount by the hearth. Suspended at the moment, a choice hung in the air—acknowledge or ignore. Electing the latter, the siblings returned to their tasks, seeking refuge in the mundane, leaving the mysterious presence lurking in the shadows unaddressed, a curiosity yet to be unraveled.

Ghostly Watcher

Late afternoon, the oppressive heat of summertime lingered in the air, casting long shadows across the living room. Emmie and her little brother Anton, aged 12 and 14, were nestled comfortably on the vast expanse of the oversized couch, fixated on the epic adventures unfolding on the colossal television screen. With rapt attention, they watched their favorite Digimon characters, each occupying one of the three cushions that spanned the width of the couch.

Anton sat closest to the TV, his eyes locked onto the animated world before him, while Emmie reclined at the opposite end, her gaze transfixed on the unfolding saga. But as the storyline grew more intense, a spooky sensation overcame her. It started subtly, like a faint whisper of unease, as if an invisible force tugged at her from beneath.

Slowly but surely, Emmie felt herself sinking toward the center of the couch, the soft cushions seemingly engulfing her with an eerie persistence. Her heart quickened as she attempted to resist the inexorable pull. Still, it was as if someone heavy, something inexplicable, was slowly pressing down on the seat beside her, compelling her deeper into the plush embrace of the middle cushion.

Despite the growing sense of unease, Emmie tried to maintain her focus on the animated spectacle, determined not to be distracted by the bizarre phenomenon unfolding beneath her. The Digimon adventures continued to captivate Anton's attention, and it seemed he remained oblivious to the peculiar events transpiring beside him.

It wasn't until the cushions beneath her began to spring back to life, relinquishing their relentless grip, that Emmie realized the gravity of the situation. Panic surged as she turned her gaze to the space beside her. A substantial depression, as if an invisible presence had just vacated its seat, remained an unnerving testament to the inexplicable.

Emmie stole a furtive glance at her brother, who remained engrossed in the onscreen action. Unspoken words hung heavy in the air. A silent pact between siblings bound them to secrecy regarding these strange occurrences. It was a chilling encounter that would linger in their memories, a pact of silence forged in the face of the unexplainable and a mystery that they dared not confront directly.

Roswell Parallel Universe

When Emmie was a young teen, she began suffering from reoccurring nightmares, each more terrifying than the last. She found herself in someone else's body in these dreams, living through their harrowing experiences. She could feel pain, fear, and the injuries. The dreams always centered around an alien invasion, a relentless onslaught threatening humanity. These haunting dreams were an unrelenting descent into surreal terror, their vibrancy surreal after waking.

Emmie couldn't forget the fear that they might wrench her life from her grasp, leaving her to die of sheer fright. She worried they were for someone, even if they weren't for her. Whom she couldn't say. Born and raised in Roswell, New Mexico, a town forever associated with tales of extraterrestrial encounters, Emmie considered these dreams connected to her hometown's paranormal aura.

These dreams occurred over several years in six episodes in which she experienced life within the body of a teenage girl with a family like hers, with a younger brother and two parents. Their home resembled hers.

Part One: The Dissension

Initially, she was awakened by a blinding light passing by her window. Emmie stumbled out of bed. The light flashed as if coming from the front yard. She walked out into the living room, clad only in a tee-shirt. Sleepily, she stared out of the bay window overlooking the field, seeing what looked like searching floodlights flashing around.

Startled by a clatter of dishes in the dining room, she saw her brother sitting at the kitchen table, finishing a bowl of cereal. Midnight snacking was something he was regularly guilty of. She was thankful that the startling sound was so innocent. She reached the table, leaning, futilely attempting to ground herself. She sat with her brother, telling him about the strange light. Together, they looked out the dining room window, deliberating over what the lights could be. They noticed the beams descending from hovering vehicles, shooting lasers at everything that moved. They heard a blood-curdling scream come from someone down the road. The gravity of the situation made her blood run cold.

Several spotlights pierced the darkness without warning, flooding the kitchen with their blinding glow. Terrified, they hid beneath the table as the search lights swept over the room, casting shadows and filling it with a terrifying luminescence. Anton, as stiff as a board, reached for his sister. They sat huddled, wrapped up together. Trembling, Emmie peered down the hallway, where the light, now having moved from the front of the house to the east side, illuminated her parents' room. She could see the light flash from under the bedroom door.

The kitchen flooded in the safety of darkness. She summoned the courage to dart down the hall to her parents' door. It was locked. Panic surged through her as she banged on the door. No one answered. She picked the lock, bursting into the room. Empty, a disheveled bed. No parents in sight. Vanished.

Rushing back to the kitchen, she discovered her brother was gone. The unsettling sounds of unknown creatures prowling outside the house intensified her dread. She ducked back down, listening to the nightmarish cacophony. Eyes squeezed tight, wishing away this turn of events, her ears tuned into a chorus of screams and ammunition shots echoing in the distance.

Summoning courage, Emmie decided to escape. Grabbing car keys, she slipped out into the night. Blood pumping, she pressed her body against the house, racing toward the car. Creeping and then sprinting, I made it inside. Too afraid to look around, hunkered down, feeling for the ignition. She heard something scraping nearby. Daring a peek, she spotted her mother huddled up in a fetal position on the ground, in just a flimsy nightgown, hair wild. She was weeping and muttering to herself.

"Mom!" Emmie called quietly, but the woman wasn't responding. Deep breath, she set down the keys and crawled out of the car. Touching her mother's arm, the woman began to shriek.

"No," Emmie growled, clapping her hand over her mother's mouth. She tried encouraging the woman to get up but was not getting through a frightened animal. The daughter began to drag her mother by her elbow the ten feet of the car. She opened the back door, and the woman half crawled into the vehicle, beginning to wail loudly. Emmie looked around in alarm, afraid that this mad woman was giving away their location.

Jumping back into the driver's seat, fumbled with the keys. Something ran, slamming into the passenger with terrifying speed, wrenching it open. It was her brother. He clambered into the front passenger seat of the car.

"Drive!" he squealed. Emmie hit the gas, but the emergency brake was on, and she just peeled out. "Do you even know how?" he followed in apprehension

"Better than you," she retorted, releasing the brake and throwing the car into reverse. As she tapped the brakes, the lights illuminated a whole army of alien creatures standing sentry, impeding her path. She gunned it, running half a dozen down, the car bumping as they heard groaning and popping underneath the tires. She slammed on the brakes and threw it into drive, feeling like a character in one of her apocalypse shows. She had to do this, she told herself. A cat was skittering across the road, and a spattering of little beings running toward them. She sped forward without concern for any life except those in the car.

"Dad!" Anton wailed, beginning to cry, turning back and looking at the house under the glow of searchlights.

"We have to go," Emmie told him matter-of-factly, knowing that their dad had the best chance of survival, being the largest and strongest of them. She couldn't get distracted by wondering where he was. She reasoned that he would want them to escape.

"Honey?" her mother cried, half coming to her senses.

"Do you see your dad?" she asked her son, opening the back door and looking out.

"No, Mom!" Emmie yelled as she saw her mother maniacally leaning out the car door. As they passed one of the creatures, it grabbed the woman's long, flowing hair, grasping it and wrenching her down.

"Mom!" Emmie shrieked, reaching behind her, trying to pull the woman back in while still driving through a battlefield. Her mother, in a demented state, locked eyes with her daughter as the nightmarish creatures outside dragged her away.

"No." Anton squeaked timidly as he sunk back into his seat. Emmie reached the highway and headed north out of town. The kids could see the city engulfed in flames and strange flying crafts poised overhead, shooting without discretion. Emmie had no choice but to gun it, leaving behind all she knew in a nightmare burning down. The ordeal was far from over, and their survival was now her only concern.

She woke, feeling like her heart may burst out of her chest. About a year later, she dreamt the following.

Part 2: Stranded and Unarmed

Emmie drove through the night with no one but her brother by her side, the car stained with blood and bodily debris from the chaos. The city was ablaze, and flying crafts filled the skies. Fear clung to her as they sped away from the devastation.

She drove even when she was dozing and swerving off the road. Pinching herself until she drew blood, she drove on. As dawn broke, they ran out of gas and sought refuge under a forsaken underpass. As the day passed and the day turned to night, hunger gnawed at their stomachs, and thirst parched their throats. With no supplies, they huddled barefoot, hiding from the unknown horrors lurking beyond the concrete shadows.

Exhausted and terrified, they eventually drifted into fitful sleep, their dreams filled with haunting visions of the unfolding nightmarish events. Every moment of respite was plagued by the memory of their mother's fate, the blood-soaked car, not knowing what had happened to their father, their pets, their friends, and the unconceivable pandemonium.

She woke up and dreamt the next part three months later.

Part 3: A Flicker of Hope

Days turned into months as Emmie and her brother clung to survival, scavenging for food and water, their pajamas and bare feet ill-suited for the harsh reality of their new world—the pillaged clothes and necessities wherever they could be found. The children found old places to camp but mostly hid, desperately waiting each day for the cover of darkness.

While walking down the highway, a family van approached them. They were saddled with an empty canteen, a ragged backpack, and comic books. Although on guard, this was their first human sighting, which offered a glimmer of hope. A man, a woman, and a little boy, around eight years old, beckoned the siblings to join them. Starving and weary, Emmie was tempted by the promise of food and safety. The people assured them they were from a group, which was a safe harbor for five other families.

The group took them in, offering shelter, sustenance, and a sense of belonging. Emmie's gratitude was immense. She began to rebuild her trust in humanity. She and Anton slept on the great room floor with a dozen others.

Together, they formed a fragile community. Having eaten, bathed, and slept, she was skeptical of this merciful turn of events but grateful nonetheless. She spoke with the others and heard their stories. Anton told them theirs. There was a kid with a few toys that was playing with him. She smiled, watching her brother act like a kid again as she hugged a pillow for reassurance. The memory of her mother's face being dragged out of the car flashed into her mind. She squeezed her eyes tight. She was glad to see Anton adjusting so well when she opened them. She noticed the windows covered in foil with sheets shrouding them further to ward off prying eyes.

As the first few days passed, Emmie's intuition began to prick. Late the next night, she heard a puzzling noise from another room as she prepared for bed. She couldn't ignore her suspicion.

To her horror, she discovered the man and woman speaking in an incomprehensible language, an alien tongue that made her hair stand up. Peering around the corner, she witnessed their distorted reflections in a mirror, their true forms hidden beneath human appearance.

The illusion shattered. Emmie knew she had to escape the sinister clutches of these interlopers.

She woke and dreamt the next part a week later.

Part 4: A Desperate Flight

Emmie could no longer ignore the truth; their sanctuary was not what it seemed. The family that had offered her shelter was, in reality, something hellish, speaking in an alien tongue that frightened her to her very core. Her essence screamed at her to escape. Waiting for the group to fall asleep, resolve steeled, she made her move. She slipped out of her sleeping spot and tiptoed through the quiet house, a moving shadow.

Needing to escape these imposters woke Anton soundlessly. She laid a finger over her lips and signaled him to follow. His friend also woke, and Anton told him to stay silent while they escaped. They crept over the others. With her heart in her throat, Emmie opened the front door, careful not to make a sound. The night air was cool and foreboding, but she couldn't let fear deter her. Breaths in shallow gasps, she guided the two kids into the darkness.

Suddenly, her instincts kicked in, and she realized she couldn't trust anyone, not even the little boy who had seemed so innocent. She reluctantly let go of his hand, scooped up Anton, tossed him over her shoulder, and ran out into the woods. She watched the smaller child disappear into the treacherous night, her guts twisting in guilt. Here, she woke up with tear-streaked cheeks. She dreamt of the next part the following fall.

Part 5: Pursuit in the Shadows

Emmie's footsteps crunched through foliage as she loped further away from the house. Senses on high alert. Each rustle of leaves and distant sound tied her stomach in knots. She knew they would come for them. They had to keep moving. Sweat-soak, her damp shirt clung as she navigated the moonlit terrain. She could feel the presence of her pursuers drawing closer. Desperation fueled her steps, her breaths ragged. She let Anton down, and he ran beside her as the pair fled deeper into the wilderness.

A group of aliens shattered the silence in an encampment, their strange language infesting the darkness. Emmie stifled a cough. The night erupted into violence. Her throat was dry as she sprinted through the underbrush, her bare feet slapping against the unforgiving ground in the opposite direction. The creatures gave chase.

She woke sweat-drenched and dreamt the next part three nights later.

Part 6: A Terrifying Revelation

Emmie's flight through the night felt endless, her body pushed to its limits. Tasting blood in her mouth, she knew she couldn't run forever. Exhaustion consumed made a desperate call. She collapsed, hiding in the brush, hoping her pursuers wouldn't find her. She looked beside her and saw she had lost Anton in her mad flight. Pressing her fingers into her eyes to stifle the flow of hot tears. She covered her mouth, gasping in horror.

Minutes stretched into hours. She dared not move. Breath pent up in anticipation. Then, she heard the sound of three-toed footsteps drawing near. Panic surged up within her, knowing they were closing in. Upon her before she could decide whether or not to bolt. Their grotesque forms loomed in the moonlight; their true nature revealed in all its horrifying glory.

They weren't the small, soft-bodied beings that were previously portrayed. They were large, thorny parasites infiltrating the lives of humans. The spawn embodies a meld of decaying flesh and oozing slime covered in a mucus-like membrane that exudes a vile, greenish-blue phosphorescent slime. As it moves, nauseating undulations cause the slime to slosh and squelch. Beneath the translucent membrane, wriggling tendrils writhe, and its limbs resemble grotesque tentacles and skeletal arms adorned with jagged protrusions. Its form features a pulsating, featureless mass sporadically revealing a fanged maw lined with razor-sharp teeth emitting a vile stench of sweet rotting meat and sulfur. Crimson, luminescent eyes intermittently pierce the darkness. Victims, locked in its sight, are subjected to an indescribable symphony of agonized wails, discordant whispers, and unsettling screeches that penetrate minds.

Once locked in its gaze, the abominable maggot-like beast emits a discordant symphony of sounds that defy description, agonized wails, dissonant whispers, and a screech of cosmic horrors. Victims who encounter the monstrosity in its proper form are gripped by a terror that consumes their sanity, leaving them in perpetual dread. Any flora or fauna unfortunate enough to be in its proximity is microwaved, withers, and dies, reduced to ashen husks.

As it moves, it leaves a trail of cosmic distortion and warped reality, bending light and space to create disorienting illusions that further terrify and confuse anyone. Having encountered this entity face-to-face, Emmie has been forever haunted by the indescribable horror they've witnessed. It is a being from the bottomless voids of the universe, a harbinger of existential dread, and a testament to the unfathomable terrors that await in the cosmic abyss.

With a gut-wrenching scream, Emmie woke from her nightmare. Heart palpitating, she clutched her bruised arm, a painful reminder of the dream's reality. The aliens had invaded her dreams once more, leaving her traumatized. As she lay in bed, the memories of her dream-world ordeal lingered. She believed these nightmares were more than mere dreams. Living in Roswell, she had become intimately familiar with the town's alien legends.

Still, she wondered if her recurring nightmares were a terrifying glimpse into an otherworldly reality slowly bleeding into her own. Emmie's life in Roswell, New Mexico, was forever changed by her nightmarish experiences. Her dreams, once innocuous, had become a portal to a horrifying parallel world, one where aliens invaded the lives of innocent humans, revealing their true parasitic nature. In the shadow of the past, Emmie's life had become a living nightmare, where the unknown horrors of the cosmos bled into her waking world, and the town's infamous legends took on a chilling new significance.

Beelzebub

In the faraway land of the Philippines, where the air was thick with secrets and the moon cast long shadows, TJ Babac shared a room with his little sister, Angel. Their world was defined by the mysteries that unfurled in the still of bedtime when their imaginations danced with imagination. TJ gently prodded his sister to sleep one night as the hour grew late. As she settled into her sheets, her wide-eyed innocence transformed into a sudden, alarmed gaze. With a hushed hiss, she pointed a trembling finger to the darkened corner of the room, where an ominous, shadowy figure loomed.

"What's that?" she whispered, her voice quivering with fascination and terror. Both siblings fixated on the chilling silhouette, its form seemingly forged from the very essence of darkness.

"Is that the devil?" she asked tremblingly as she noticed the diabolical horns that crowned the shadowy specter. Fear pulsed through her veins like an electric shock, and she turned to her older brother for reassurance.

Though gripped by his fear, TJ summoned every ounce of courage he possessed. He leaned in close, his words soft and soothing as he sought to quell the sinister apparition. "It's just your imagination," he whispered, his voice trembling slightly. "Go to sleep. It's nothing to be afraid of."

As if in response to his words, the menacing figure faded a moment later, its ominous presence dissipating like smoke in the wind. The room was once again cloaked in the ordinary darkness of their childhood bedroom. But the memory of that night, of the sinister shadow with its eerie horns, would forever haunt TJ and his sister. It was a tale they would share with trembling voices and wide-eyed disbelief, a story of a chilling visitation from the unknown seared into their memories like a nightmare that lingered long after dawn had broken.

Endless Night

In the heart of the Philippines, beneath a sky of a thousand stars, TJ and his friends embarked on a nocturnal adventure that would test the boundaries of their reality. Full of youthful exuberance, teenagers chased the sparkling city's allure, eager to paint the town red in the obsidian canvas of the night.

The winding roads were as familiar as the lines of an old friend's face. The night air was filled with the promise of adventure, and the engine's purr sang a sweet serenade as they left their hometown behind. Destination: the next city over.

As the minutes stretched into hours, they curiously failed to reach their intended destination. Perplexity seized them as they found themselves on a street that bore a haunting resemblance to the one they had left behind the hour prior. They had returned to their starting point. Baffled but undeterred, they turned the car around, determined to escape this disorienting déjà vu. But fate seemed to conspire against them. Once again, they retraced their steps like the roads beneath their tires held them prisoner.

A chilling realization struck one of them. Despite their belief that they were traveling in a straight line, they were ensnared in the clutches of a maddening loop, condemned to circle in the familiar terrain that defied their understanding endlessly. The sixth time they passed a distinctive house that seemed to taunt them with its familiarity, they fell into a deep, contemplative conversation. They pondered the enigma that held them captive, their voices trembling with uncertainty. Why had this befallen them, and how could they break free from its relentless grasp?

Desperation drove them to make futile attempts to escape, veering off down different roads, attempting to return to their homes, only to be met with the same disheartening result. Each path led inexorably back to its starting point. After the eighth bewildering cycle, hope emerged on the horizon. Somehow, inexplicably, they broke free from the relentless loop that had ensnared them. The familiar landscape gave way to new terrain, and once an oppressive shroud, the night now offered a path toward salvation.

Finally free, they made their way back home. The memory of that night lingered. The endless night tested their resolve, challenged their understanding, and left them with an unshakeable sense that they had ventured into the uncharted realms of time. It was a tale they would recount in hushed tones, forever haunted by the enigma of their journey through the Twilight Zone.

Astral Projection University

During their college years, Emmie and her boyfriend, TJ, studied late into the night in TJ's cramped dorm room. The dismally lit space seemed worlds away from the bustling campus, and as the clock inched past midnight, TJ resigned to rest. Kissing Emmie on the forehead, brushed his teeth and fell immediately into a deep sleep. By 3 am, exhaustion began to claw at her senses.

A tiny kitchenette spilled into a modest living room near the front door. The pièce de résistance was a large mirror mounted on the living room wall, a reflective surface that framed the bedroom door, the adjacent hallway, and the entrance to the bathroom. Emmie was listening to "Thunder" by 'Imagine Dragons' on her phone when she saw a flash saying that her battery was low on juice.
In search of her phone charger, Emmie tiptoed into the bedroom, where the soft rhythm of TJ's breathing resonated. He lay sprawled on the bed, already lost in the depths of dreamland. Returning to her spot at the coffee table, she resumed her study session, determined to conquer the late-night workload. As minutes stretched into a quarter-hour, an odd sensation began to creep over her, a numbness tingling through her limbs, akin to the fluttering wings of a thousand butterflies.

Her gaze drifted to the glass coffee table. She saw movement in the reflection. A figure, long and tall, shifted from the bedroom to the bathroom. The assumption that TJ had stirred from his slumber when he was sleeping so hard surprised her, but she remained focused. The bathroom remained shrouded in darkness; its light stubbornly refused to pierce the obscurity.

Emmie, immersed in her work, pushed the encounter from her mind. Slumping forward, obscuring her view of the daunting mirror, her thoughts colliding with deadlines and equations. Unexplained terrors weren't finished with her. Once more, a chilling sensation clung to her. Eyes transfixed on the computer screen, she caught a glimpse of movement in its reflection. A gray apparition emerged in the mirrored display.

A hand raised, fingers grazing the kitchen counters in a spectral dance that persisted for an eternity before vanishing into the bedroom's shadowy embrace. Emmie's pulse quickened as she watched the figure's baffling circuit from bathroom to bedroom, bedroom to kitchen, and then back again.

Summoning her courage, she ventured into the bedroom, her words trembling as she whispered to the peacefully resting TJ, seeking reassurance that everything was as it should be. The weight of strangeness pressed upon her as she gazed upon his still form. He lay sprawled on his stomach, one arm lackadaisically extending from beneath the pillow, an image that should have brought warmth but now caused her alarm. He seemed almost lifeless. Feeling his cheek, he was warm, and she saw his eyelids flutter. He was sleeping peacefully. She chastised herself for being a scaredy cat and returned to her workstation.

Sitting back down, Emmie's eyes were drawn again to the ominous mirror in the living room. The figure, with its ghostly grace, reappeared. This time, it lingered, just standing as if it was watching her. She kept her eyes transfixed on her monitor and turned up Bad Liar by Imagine Dragons, refusing to acknowledge the apparition. When it finally faded away. She slapped her computer closed and ran back to the bedroom.

She shook TJ gently, desperation in her voice, but he remained tangled in his dreams. Knowing she was tired and possibly out of her mind, she crawled under the blankets, wrapped around him like a spider monkey, and, relaxing, fell asleep. Morning would bring a revelation.

They woke early for class as dawn's first light kissed their dorm room. He began to share that he was having the strangest dream. He dreamt that Emmie was still studying and that he got up to go to the bathroom and became confused. Disoriented, he went back and forth a few times and then came back and laid down. TJ continued dreaming later that he was hungry. So, he went to the kitchen to get a snack but couldn't open the cabinets. He could see Emmie studying. He said he could hear Imagine Dragons playing from her earbuds. He reached for her, asking for help, but couldn't walk over to her. He stood reaching for her until he could move again. Feeling fatigued, he looked at the microwave and saw it was already three. He floated back to bed.

The time he saw on the microwave clock matched the hour when Emmie had witnessed the spooky apparition. Chills coursed through them both, and the puzzling events of that night remained etched in their memories. This enigma was an astral projection that left them questioning the boundaries of reality and dreams.

Satan in the Fire

In the winter of 2019, TJ and his family were adjusting to life in the United States. They had moved into the Vista del Rio Apartment complex in Carlsbad, New Mexico. The family consisted of TJ, his mother, May, his father, Bernard, his younger brother Jasir, and his little sister Angel.
TJ was asleep one chilly December night when a peculiar sound disrupted his dreams. He stirred, brow furrowing in confusion, and strained his ears to identify the enigmatic noise. At first, he couldn't quite place it, but a curious smile spread across his face as it intensified. It sounded like the cries of a newborn baby, and he wondered who in the complex had recently become a parent.

However, an uneasy feeling crept over him as he listened more closely. The sound was coming from just one room over, from Jasir's bedroom. He turned and noticed an odd blue light from the hallway, casting shadows on the walls.

TJ's anxiety increased. His palms began to sweat as he felt a presence he couldn't explain. He squeezed his eyes shut, hoping that whatever it was would disappear. But the crying entity seemed to enter the hall and enter his room. Lying on his side, he pretended to be asleep, trying to ignore it.

The crying sound inched closer until it blasted directly into his ear, and the room fell silent. TJ could sense a warmth, like hot breath, on the back of his neck, and he remained frozen in fear. Softly at first, a demonic laugh emanated from the entity, causing the hairs on his arms to stand on end. Still, he resisted reacting.

When the demon realized its taunts were in vain, it began to tap TJ's shoulder. Fear surged through him, but he could still move, ruling out the possibility of sleep paralysis. Desperate to escape the torment, he rolled over to evade the tapping finger, but it moved to his other shoulder.

The entity started whispering ominous, ancient phrases and hissing while chanting obscenities in a language TJ couldn't understand. The warmth from it grew unbearable, and he forced his eyes shut even tighter. With his eyes closed, he was consumed by a vivid vision of the room turning red, the demon pointing skyward, and TJ beginning to levitate, leaving his body behind.

He saw pits of tortured souls, their screams piercing the air while the satanic figure laughed maniacally. Hot air blew past him, and his skin broke out in a cold sweat. After a harrowing tour of the underworld, the descent began. He felt the soothing cool of his bedroom returning. The tormenting screams faded away.

After five minutes of blessed solace, TJ summoned the courage to open his eyes. He was back in his room, safely in his bed, alone. His body was drenched in sweat. Parched, he noticed bruises on both of his shoulders, a painful reminder of the relentless jabbing from the demon.

Terrified and desperate for answers, TJ rushed to his parents' room and pounded on the door. He recounted the horrifying ordeal, and his parents listened with mild concern. TJ was told it was just a case of sleep paralysis and encouraged to sleep with his siblings for comfort. The next day, his father placed protective herbs in each room to ward off sinister actions. However, the memory of that night haunted him.

Months later, after the family had moved out, their former apartment mysteriously caught fire. Of all the units in the complex, only TJ's eight-unit building was consumed by the flames. It was later demolished on April 12, 2021, and the cause of the fire remained a perplexing mystery, forever intertwined with the inexplicable events of that chilling night.

Doppelganger of Quezon City

In 2014, during high school, TJ was caught in a chilling experience with his schoolmates. The setting was a five-story school in Quezon City, Philippines that TJ and his classmates attended. After the final bell had rung at 5 pm, TJ and his friends decided to hang out on the top story of the building. It was an extraordinary evening to have the campus mostly abandoned due to the upcoming holiday. They relished the rare opportunity to have the entire floor to themselves. The kids wrestled, teased each other about girls, and complained about their math teacher.

As the minutes ticked by, Patrick said his phone was dying. His mom liked always to be able to reach him. He had to head home. The group said goodbye and continued to chat and enjoy their afternoon. Thirty minutes after Patrick had left, the boys were people-watching near a window, their laughter echoing through the empty halls. Suddenly, their mirth abruptly stopped as they saw something curious. On the basketball court below, they spotted Patrick, or at least, it appeared to be. He was wearing the same clothes he wore when he left, including his collector's cap that was a limited edition, shooting hoops in just the style Patrick always did. There was no mistaking his familiar silhouette. The group began yelling at him.

"Patrick! We thought you went home!" they called down, their voices echoing in the stillness of the evening. But to their bewilderment, the figure on the court looked up at them, revealing Patrick's face with a blank expression. It dropped the ball and began to head towards the gate briskly as if driven by some unspoken urgency. Their calls grew more frantic as they pleaded for an explanation, but the figure remained unresponsive, as though it hadn't heard them at all.

Confused, they called Patrick. His cell went to voicemail. TJ called his house phone. To their shock, Patrick answered the call and confirmed that he had been home for nearly an hour. He couldn't be at the basketball court; he was making noodles.

Disbelief bathed TJ and his friends as the reality of the situation sank in. What they had witnessed was nothing short of a doppelganger, a duplicate impersonation of their friend, a supernatural presence that had mimicked Patrick's appearance and movements with startling precision. Terrified and with no rational explanation to cling to, they quickly made their way home, haunted by the encounter. The memory of that evening would forever serve as a reminder that sometimes, reality can take on a chilling and otherworldly twist, defying all that we think we understand about the world.

Light Over Alien Country

In 2018, while living in Carlsbad, New Mexico, TJ finished his shift at Starbucks, with the clock ticking well past 11:30 pm. Wide awake, he asked two coworkers if they wanted to hang out before going home. Emily and Anikin suggested they cruise outside the city to stargaze.

They embarked on a leisurely drive, cruising through the winding roads that led them up a hill. Their aim was simple: to relax and enjoy each other's company in the night's quietude beneath the vast and starry expanse of alien country not far from the infamous Roswell, New Mexico. As they meandered uphill, an unexpected sight shattered the tranquil ambiance.

A deer darted across the road; its silhouette illuminated by the headlights of TJ's car. The trio watched as the creature vanished into the obscurity of the night. As they descended the hill, their attention was drawn to the heavens. High above them, in the expansive night sky of this mysterious and otherworldly region, something extraordinary occurred. A luminous streak, akin to a shooting star but unlike any they had ever seen, blazed across the sky. The brilliance of the celestial phenomenon left them spellbound. It lit up the whole atmosphere and hung there.

With a sense of wonder, TJ described the light as a vivid shade of green. Beside him, Anikin's eyes blinked, arguing that it was a striking shade of blue. Emily, equally mesmerized, observed the celestial enigma in a soft, radiant yellow. After commenting and realizing that each had observed a different sight, they were perplexed and exhilarated. The trio exchanged incredulous glances, struggling to make sense of the inexplicable spectacle witnessed. They recounted their perceptions, each insisting that their color was accurate.

Then, as swiftly as it had appeared, the mysterious light vanished, disappearing into the vast expanse of the night in the blink of an eye. Left in its wake was a sense of. To this day, TJ, Anikin, and Emily remain unable to explain how they all saw the same celestial phenomenon together yet carried away distinctly different memories and perceptions. It remains a lingering mystery, a testament to the wonders in the quiet depths of space, especially in the land of alien folklore near Roswell, New Mexico.

Haunted Lee House in Black Forest

On another adventure, Dimitris and Ian decided to visit Colorado's famous Lee House, nestled in the Black Forest that was featured on the show Sightings. Here's how that story goes.

In 1990, the Lee family embarked on a journey filled with dread as they moved into a log cabin home nestled deep within the foreboding Black Forest of Colorado. Little did they know that this seemingly idyllic abode would soon become the epicenter of unexplainable and sinister occurrences.

The first unsettling signs emerged as the Lee family assumed ownership of the cabin. Electronics began to malfunction, mysterious lights flickered in the darkest corners of the home, and eerie sounds echoed through its timeworn walls. But these were only the prelude to the true horrors that awaited them.

The Lee children, innocent and curious, were the first to witness the shadowy figures lurking within the dense forest surrounding their homes. These spectral intruders watched from the shadows, accompanied by a noxious odor that clawed at the family's senses, burning their eyes, noses, and throats.

Desperate to make sense of the inexplicable, Steven Lee installed security cameras throughout the cabin. However, these cameras only served to deepen the mystery. Motion detectors triggered sporadically, recording over 60 unsettling events that mimicked break-ins but yielded no evidence of theft. Instead, the recordings captured bizarre phenomena—floating orbs, flashes of light, and chilling apparitions that defied explanation.

The paranormal activity escalated when the renowned investigative show "Sightings" documented the strange events plaguing the Lee family. During their stay, the crew reported several eerie interactions and even an attempted possession. A psychic at the scene revealed a disturbing truth—the property harbored a rift in space-time, trapping numerous spirits in its eerie grasp. Among them was a young boy known to the Lee family, whose death had been officially ruled a suicide. However, the boy's restless spirit wished to convey a chilling revelation—he had been murdered.

Driven by their curiosity and a desire to experience the supernatural firsthand, Dimitris and Ian embarked on their adventure to the site. Hundreds of years before the cabin's existence, the area had been a haunting ground for accused witches, subjected to cruel punishments like burning at the stake or forced exile, a sentence to fend for themselves in the wilderness.

Furthermore, this region had been part of the Oregon Trail, a historic westward migration route in the 19th century notorious for its arduous and perilous journey. The pioneers who braved this trail faced many deadly challenges, including disease, accidents, starvation, harsh weather, and encounters with indigenous peoples. Death and suffering had left their mark on this land, with countless lives lost and unburied.

Driving home from a barbecue one night, Ian had a mysterious encounter with a ghostly woman along the road. He was in traffic, and the streets were wet. He wasn't able to investigate but told Dimitris about it. After researching the area and discovering its reputation as a paranormal hotspot, a group decided to delve deeper into its mysteries.

Dimitris, Ian, and another friend drove into the Black Forest. Arriving at the Lee House, they were immediately oppressed by an otherworldly energy. What was once a comfortable evening suddenly turned cold and clammy. The air grew thick with tension as a dense fog rolled in, casting a gray pall over the surroundings. They were drawn deeper into the forest.

Strange lights, unlike any headlights, danced before them. But the lights above began to explode in bursts of brilliance, resembling fireworks on the Fourth of July. Visions unfolded before their eyes, and a beaten woman hitchhiking alongside the road, a crashed semi-truck in a ditch. The woman was hit and killed. Their senses were overwhelmed as a colossal, shadowy figure with a seven-foot wingspan swooped low over their heads, causing them to cower in fear.

The forest seemed to hold its breath. The cicadas fell silent, and the wind ceased to rustle through the trees. The flutter of owls went still. Like a phantom emerging from the darkest recesses of their nightmares, they saw her, the Wailing Widow. Draped in a long, flowing gown, her face locked in a deathly gaze, she approached them, each step measured and chilling.

Time seemed to stand still as the phantasm drew nearer, her eyes pricking their souls. She grew closer and closer and seemed to be mouthing a cautionary tale, yet she made no sound. Without warning, she vanished into the ether, leaving the trio utterly bewildered and terrified.

Fear coursing through their veins, Dimitris, Ian, and their third wasted no time. They hastily retreated to their vehicle and sped away from the Black Forest, the fright they encountered escorting them out of the woods.

As they rejoined the highway, they felt a sense of relief, thankful for the breath in their lungs and the safety of the world outside that forsaken place. In this world, the chilling presence of the Wailing Widow, the countless lost souls of the Oregon Trail, and the soulless spirits of the Lee Cabin were left behind, if only for a time.

Nightmare in Rolling Hills Asylum

In a chilling escapade, Dimitris and his then-girlfriend, Cherie, dared to tread into the darkness of the Haunted Rolling Hills Asylum in Batavia, New York. Once a humble working farm, this historical structure had transformed into the Genesee County Poor House in 1827—a supposed refuge for society's unfortunate souls. However, behind the facade of charity lay the grim reality of indentured servitude and cruelty. Within its walls, widows, orphans, and the mentally ill intermingled while unclaimed bodies were unrested in unmarked graves. Worst of all, the asylum played host to Batavia's mentally ill, subjected to the malevolent whims of mad scientists with a penchant for sadistic experimentation. With over 1,700 documented deaths and countless others lost to history, it ranked the second most haunted site in the United States.

In 2016, Dimitris and Cherie embarked on a haunting adventure, attending a guided tour of the infamous Rolling Hills Asylum. Armed only with flashlights, they delved into the sinister depths of this haunted place. The tour led them down dim, drafty corridors, past the forlorn remnants of patient rooms, and towards eerie displays of medieval medical instruments, instruments of torment. With audacious temerity, they dared to sit in one of the wretched wheelchairs that had once been tools of persecution. Snapshots were taken in the hope of capturing spectral entities, all while oblivious to the looming darkness that threatened to consume their feeble lights.

Then, without warning, their flashlights began to flicker in eerie synchrony. Dimitris, recognizing an opportunity to contact the other side, activated his audio recorder to capture several minutes of their eerie surroundings. They sought answers to the enigma that had turned their lights into playthings.

The tour concluded, and they reluctantly departed, taking a few photographs as keepsakes to immortalize their chilling adventure. As they embarked on the journey home, Dimitris decided to play back the audio recording, the vehicle's interior steeped in an anticipatory silence. Suddenly, a bone-chilling, blood-curdling shriek erupted from the recorder—an agonizing cry that parched their mouths, curdled their stomachs, drained color from their faces, and sent shivers coursing through their spines. It was a wail that seemed to carry the weight of unspeakable horrors endured. The listeners could scarcely fathom the torment that had befallen the person behind that voice. They pulled over on the side of the road, their bodies covered in goosebumps, their hearts pounding with trepidation.

Playing the recording again, the haunting wail clawed its way through the vehicle's speakers. It was the voice of a woman whose existence had been brutally snuffed out cruelly. Her lament faded into the cold night, and Dimitris and Cherie couldn't help but imagine the harrowing final moments of her life.

They sat there, stranded on the desolate roadside, their senses tinged with anxiety, pondering the identity of this tormented soul and the sinister fate that had befallen her. The mysteries of the Rolling Hills Asylum had burrowed deeper into their souls, leaving them with more questions than answers and a chilling encounter forever in their memories.

Wicked Wendy

Dimitris, now married to a woman named Keea with two beautiful kids, lives in a beautiful two-story home in Maricopa, Arizona. He has a little girl named Alethea and a baby named Tommy. Ali was getting near to school age. She spent her days chasing her brother around the house, playing with dolls, spending time in her jungle gym, and splashing in her swimming pool in the idyllic backyard.

All was well until things began to go wrong in the Rentzios household. Dimitris and his wife started noticing that instead of playing in the jungle gym on the grassy knoll, she was sitting in the corner by herself, facing the fence, playing calmly in the gravel. This seemed an odd choice of activities since she had all the most coveted toys for which her heart had desired. Instead of playing with her favorite things, her beloved toys were carelessly strewn all over the yard, completely ignored.

"Dimitris, what's Ali doing?" He asked his wife.

"I have no idea. She's been spending all of her time in that corner recently."

"Weird," he puzzled. He went out back and approached his daughter. He was surprised when she acted like he was interrupting a conversation.

"What are you up to, Ali?" her father asked.

"Nothing, Daddy."

"Let's go inside," he said, holding his hand out.

"Okay," she smiled, putting her tiny hand in his, and they went in.

They ate dinner, and that night, while Keea was bathing Ali, her mother asked her about the new game she'd been playing.

"What game?" Ali asked.

"In the backyard," Keea nudged.

"Oh! I was playing with my Wendy," she illuminated.

"I see," her mother said, nodding.

That night, when Keea and Dimitris were in bed talking about Wendy, they talked about how she never had any other imaginary friends, but then again, she was only four. This was likely something she would outgrow.

The following day, their parents watched as Ali ran outside to play. She ran straight to the swings, scooted on, and pumped her legs, swinging higher. Then she turned toward the fence when she heard someone call her name. There was Wendy with her strawberry-blonde hair, piercing blue eyes, and Hello Kitty shirt and denim overalls. The same shirt she always wore. Wendy was taller than Ali and older than her by a few years. Wendy knew lots of stuff, so Ali trusted her implicitly.

Keea and Dimitris watched Ali wave to the fence from the swings and run over to begin talking animatedly. Her parents looked at each other in mild alarm. Over the coming weeks, they noticed Ali spending more and more time with Wendy. When Keea's sister, Darby, came over with her black lab, Shera insistently scratched to go out back and began barking ferociously at the back fence. The entire visit, the dog stayed out back and watched that corner, at times barking and getting so worked up she was foaming at the mouth. Finally, Keea's sister left because the dog was so upset.

"It seems that Shera doesn't like Wendy," Dimitris joked that night when he and Keea were settling down for bed.

"Yeah. No kidding," his wife agreed, put off by the fact.

Saturday was Ali's fifth birthday party. Everything was in order, but Ali fell ill as soon as the guests arrived. She was weak, dizzy, and sick to her stomach. She didn't even make it out of the main room before she vomited violently. Her dad scooped her up and carried her upstairs. Her mom came up, cleaned her, and put her to bed. Dimitris told Ali to rest; they could celebrate her birthday another day.

"I never get a birthday party," Ali moaned.

"Oh, don't be silly. You have a party every year, and you'll have many more to come," her mother consoled.

"Not last year," Ali fussed. "Last year, I was sick too."

"She's right," Dimitris said. "Every year since we've lived here, Ali's gotten sick on her birthday."

"You're right. Four years in a row," Keea agreed. Why hadn't they put this together before now, they wondered. When Keea's mother, Katrina, visited the next day to check on Ali, Keea saw her staring out the back window.

"What is it, Mom?" Keea asked.

"There's a little girl out there," Katrina said. Keea pulled back the curtain and looked outside.

"Mom, there's no one there."

"She's there," Katrina assured her.

Over the month, Dimitrius and Keea began to see that Ali seemed to be arguing with Wendy and that she no longer enjoyed their playtime. More and more, they would call her away from that corner when they noticed her there and even tried to distract her outside of their home, spending more time at the park and with neighbors. Instead, Ali asked to play in her pool. When Ali tried to get in, a strong gust of wind lifted her kiddie pool filled with water up and over, and it tumbled and rolled back into that corner of the yard where Wendy stayed. Ali left her towel and went inside to play with Tommy.

One day, Dimitris found Ali crying in her bedroom. Her father picked her up, giving her one of his famous bear hugs.

"What's wrong, Love Bug?" he consoled. Wiping her eyes, she cried.

"Wendy is nasty, Daddy. She is very mean," she wept.

"Oh, no. I'm sorry. Well, sometimes friends can be mean," her dad consoled. "Maybe you just shouldn't play with Wendy anymore," he suggested.

"I don't want to. She's mad at me," she went on.

"Well, that's okay. You can play inside until she goes away," Dimitris explained. She cried until she wore herself out and was ready to lay down for a nap.

That night, when Keea was giving the kids their bath, Keea asked Ali what had happened between her and Wendy.

"Wendy's a bad girl, Mommy," explained Ali solemnly. The hair prickled on the back of Keea's neck.

"Why do you say that, Honey?" Keea probed.

"She hates you and Daddy," Ali whimpered.

"Oh?" Keea encouraged gently.

"She told me to do mean things to you and Daddy."

"Like what?" Keea asked in alarm, trying to remain calm.

"She showed me these little shells. She told me to put them in your water."

"Shells?" Keea asked. "From the yard?"

"No. That plastic shells you take from the doctor when you're sick."

"Pills?" Keea asked. "Like these?" Pulling a pill bottle from the cabinet.

"Yes." Ali began to cry. Dimitris came into the bathroom, hearing her crying.

"Oh, Ali. Wendy is very mean. Please don't listen to her," her mother said, lifting her out of the bath and into the towel D held to swaddle her.

From then on, Ali steered clear of that backyard corner, and not long after, the family moved away from the home where Wendy lived. It's been hypothesized that Wendy, jealous of Ali for having two loving parents, wished for death to befall them so that she could have a set of parents forever entrapped on the property with nothing to do but care for her.

Nightmare in Aurora

Years after both of her boys were grown, Mary Ann comfortably settled for bed in her palatial home on Easter weekend. She resided in the quiet suburbs of Aurora, Colorado, nestled amidst manicured lawns and tree-lined streets. It was well after midnight but long before dawn when she awoke with an ominous sensation. Her mouth went dry as she scanned the darkened room, senses tingling. Gasping, she saw piercing, red eyes glowing with intensity from the corner of the room.

Petrified, Mary Ann's breath quickened as a chilling presence penetrated the room. She knew not the origin of the sinister piercing eyes but knew they harbored ancient malevolence. Blood pumping, cheeks flushed, she frantically grasped for a shred of solace. Clutching her crucifix from her pendant, she prayed with fervor, first in a whisper and then aloud, invoking the power of the Lord to protect her from the unknown terror that crept upon her sanctuary.

The words of her frantic prayers filled the room. Red eyes faltered, their hostility yielding to consecrated forces. Gathering every courageous ounce of faith, Mary Ann rebuked the intruder in the name of the Lord, voice unwavering. The room quivered with an unearthly tension. Incautiously, banished by divine intervention, the crimson eyes vanished into the obscurity from whence they came.

Trembling and sweat-soaked, Mary Ann held her crucifix tightly, pulse pounding. She clutched her Bible and murmured a prayer of thanks and further protection. The ordeal ended, leaving her in a tranquil silence. She pondered the encounter, her faith secure, her understanding of the world forever altered. Once a sanctuary of comfort, the big, beautiful house in Aurora had witnessed a demonic spirit, a reminder that dark forces could touch even the most peaceful abode in the dead of night. Mary Ann, a daughter of God, knew ultimately, the light of goodness and belief in the Lord would always prevail.

Ufonautic Feline Watchers

In 2005, near Corona, New Mexico, John and Josie drove to Roswell, the site of the famed UFO crash, to visit their son, JD, and grandchildren. Driving in the grim early morning hours, the relentless journey was taking its toll after two days of non-stop travel in their motorhome. The desolate landscape stretched before them, punctuated by the occasional railroad track or remnants of long-forgotten structures.

The clock ticked toward 3 am, the world sunken into dark repose. Passing an old farmhouse, their headlights caught the attention of an unexpected presence. On the roadside sat a half-grown cat, its coat a striking black and white. Unlike any ordinary feline, it didn't scurry away or hunker in fear. Instead, it turned its head, eyes fixed upon the vehicle as it passed.

They drove on, bumping and jostling their way down the highway out of range of any radio station under a waxing moon. Strangely, another cat appeared a few miles down the road, much like the first, not walking or running away but stationary. This one was orange. Its eyes, too, followed the motorhome's passage with a calculated intensity.

As the miles rolled by, the peculiar sight repeated itself with uncanny consistency. One after another, felines black, white, others tabby, gray, and so on, stationed by the roadside. They didn't flee or behave like feral cats encountered on a highway at night. Instead, they turned their heads in unison, their eyes trained on the passing vehicle. It was an unsettling spectacle that defied expectations. After a surreal parade of twenty-five cats silently observing their journey, John turned to his wife.

"Are you seeing this?" he asked her. Josie's response confirmed the bizarre nature of the encounter.

"Yes, but I wasn't going to say anything." She replied sleepily. In that obscure stretch of the road east of Vaughn, a mysterious and unsettling procession of alienesque, feline onlookers had buried itself into their memories, and the night had unfolded in a way neither of them could have anticipated, leaving behind an indelible mark. The two were relieved to reach their destination finally and relayed the perplexing tale to the family the next day after a good, long rest.

Bigfoot of Painted Rocks Lake

In 1973, when JD was just a few months old, his parents, John and Josie, went on an unforgettable outing with his Aunt Mary Ann and Uncle Tom, an adventure. It was a crisp September day, the Montana weather finally relenting enough to take a young child outside, and the promise of a fishing trip on Painted Rocks Lake, south of Hamilton, was too enticing to resist.

The quartet shared a deep love for fishing and eagerly anticipated their day on the tranquil waters of Painted Rocks Lake. The park, snuggled in the heart of the Bitterroot Mountains, was a true gem of nature, boasting cliffs adorned with lichens in green, yellow, and orange hues, giving it the name Painted Rocks. The park sprawled across dozens of pristine acres, standing proud at nearly 5,000 feet above sea level.

After hours of casting lines into the glistening waters, hunger pangs gnawed their stomachs. Deciding to go to the shore for a well-deserved lunch break, the chosen beach was a stone's throw away from a colossal mountain that soared a hundred feet above the shoreline. Densely cloaked in twenty-foot trees, it boasted a lush and unspoiled expanse from its base to its lofty summit.

Preparing their meal, a disquiet descended upon the idyllic scene. Faint yet distinct cracking noises emanated from the pinnacle of the mountain, resembling the sound of snapping branches being cracked over a knee. Anxiety seized the party, causing them to shift their gaze toward the mountain's apex.

To their collective astonishment, the twenty-foot trees atop the mountain were parting as if forcefully shoved aside by some colossal presence. The trees bowed, creating a path of least resistance as the mysterious entity descended the hill. Panic tinged the air as their appetites vanished. Their plans for a leisurely picnic were vanquished.

Adrenaline pumping, they hastily gathered their belongings, abandoning their picnic on the ground, and scrambled back into the refuge of the boat. Urgently, they navigated it to the farthest side of the lake, putting as much distance as possible between themselves and the colossus.

From their vantage point in the middle of the lake, they beheld a distressing sight: a clear, unbroken line snaking through the trees as if a massive force had unceremoniously pushed them aside to create a trail. Their eyes strained to make out the gargantuan figure that had caused the commotion.

In the fading light, they discerned the dark, shaggy, mammoth silhouette of Bigfoot himself, drinking voraciously from the lake. He crouched down and drank on all fours from cupped hands.

He stood back up bipedally and, stretching tall, sniffed the air, looking out over the water from where they had set up their picnic. He shook his mane, hunkered down, and plodded back into the forest. The four adults sat in silence. Josie hugged her infant tight. The fear that gripped them was as vast as the wilderness surrounding them.

Vanishing Car in Casper

On a rainy night in 1989, John, Josie, and JD, now sixteen, bungled down the lonely roads of Casper, Wyoming. Exhausted from a long drive, they decided to park at a truck pullover, a lonely spot on the side of the interstate meant for resting truckers. The place offered no amenities, just a few white lines on the pavement.

The weary family settled down in the back of their van, JD reclining in the front passenger captain's chair. Sleep quickly overtook them, but tranquility was short-lived. Shaking violently, the van jolted them awake.

Bleary eyes struggling to adjust to the blinding brightness that surrounded them. Bright, flashing lights invaded their vehicle. Josie heard terrifying sounds, while John heard no sound at all. JD sat up, covering his eyes while the couple clutched each other tightly, wondering what would happen next. The lights and sounds intensified as their panic grew.

Jarred, their next memory was them barreling south down I-25, 100 miles past the truck pullover spot. Not only did they not recall the conclusion of the invasion of the lights, but they had no recollection of getting up the next day and returning to the road. Yet, here they were the next afternoon, 100 miles away. Sleep deprivation overwhelmed them. They felt as weak as if they had just swum the English Channel. They all spoke, trying to jog each other's memories for more. While neither John nor Josi could recall waking up, returning to the road, or initiating the drive onward, JD had no memory of the episode.

Catching Rainbows

In the autumn of 1985, against the backdrop of eastern Montana's endless plains, JD's curiosity was piqued by the enigmatic beauty of rainbows. Those shimmering arcs, painted across the sky when sunlight kissed raindrops, captivate him—rainbows: an illusionary multicolored arc created when light hits the water droplets from the sky. Like so many children before him, he fell under the spell of a charming yet elusive legend, the promise that a pot of gold awaited at the end of each radiant bow.

As the years rolled by, wisdom tempered the allure of folklore. JD learned that, in the eyes of science, rainbows were ethereal circles, forever out of reach. But some stories defy logic, and this is one such tale.

One drizzly day in the heart of Montana's countryside, the boy, aged twelve, was roaming the fields with his cousin Monica. The ground was moist from a rare summer rain, a delight in those sun-scorched lands outside Baker, Montana.

Monica, ever observant, called for a halt. Startled, the boy glanced down, half-expecting a hidden serpent in their path. Instead, a breathtaking sight awaited him—a narrow band of colors graced his chest, mirroring the vivid hues of a rainbow. Monica beckoned him aside, revealing that the same spectral ribbon lay upon the earth beneath their feet.

The two gazed upward, their young hearts aflutter, to behold the enchanting arc stretching from the earthly realm to the infinite heavens. It was a rainbow in all its grandeur, and it appeared as if the other end kissed the ground directly on JD's chest.

The pair scouring the terrain for thirty minutes, seeking elusive treasures. Alas, no pot of gold emerged from their quest. As the rainbow slowly faded and sunlight peeked through the thinning clouds, they retreated, their bounty a tale to be shared—a tale of chasing the rainbow's end. In that fleeting moment of youthful wonder, they left behind the whimsy and embraced a simple truth: the real treasure lay in the memories created on that drizzly Montana day, forever in their hearts

Let the Devil Take Me Tonight

In 1980, in Fairfield, North Dakota, lived the seven-year-old son of John and Josie, JD, who harbored an earnest desire always to speak the truth. However, there were times when the unvarnished truth seemed to invite a punishment far more severe than the misdeeds warranted, at least in his opinion.

JD was entangled in a web of questioning spun by his mother one afternoon. The subject of the inquiry? An elusive, perhaps imaginary, boundary known as the yard. The interrogation likely revolved around the usual parental questions: Did you brush your teeth? Did you put your dirty clothes in the hamper? Did you stay within the sacred confines of the yard'?

For this spirited child, the yard concept was a thorny issue. With an innate love for nature and a penchant for wandering freely amidst the great outdoors, the strictures of the yard were confining. He had a deep respect for the creatures of the wild- insects, reptiles, and spiders – creatures that didn't quite align with his mother's affections. Sadly, the best observation spots for these little wonders often lay beyond the yard's boundaries, as declared by their well-intentioned mother.

A clever system had been devised to navigate these boundaries. Whenever the mother exclaims JD for all to hear, it is a warning that her child has breached the perimeter and is on another expedition with moments to return with punishment. The key was to return before the ominous third call of JOHN DANIEL rang out, which typically resulted in a moderately proportionate amount of trouble. The problem was that sometimes, those elusive butterflies would lead the child on a winding path that wouldn't allow them to return in time. When his full name echoed through the neighborhood, the child and the neighbors knew that trouble was brewing.

Amidst these chases, other distractions often beckoned – dumpster diving, tree-climbing, and occasionally, the lure of the other side of Highway 85, the north-south artery bustling with speeding semis on their journey from Canada to Mexico. This treacherous road was strictly forbidden due to safety concerns. Still, sometimes, the irresistible allure of flowers on the other side was too much for the child to resist.

Highway 85 was, without a doubt, a dangerous thoroughfare. Once, a loose semi-truck tire careened off the road, crashing into the side of the local bar and embedding itself in the wall, creating an impromptu "drive-through bar." News crews flocked to the tiny town, making it the talk of North Dakota.

This particular afternoon, our young adventurer had likely followed a butterfly across the hazardous Highway 85 and miraculously returned to the yard's safety" before hearing the ominous name-calling. He believed he had safely escaped the repercussions.

Little did JD know that their astute mother was not satisfied with the interrogation. The mother, an adept detective, wanted to ascertain where her child had ventured. The boy, unable to recollect if his feet had indeed touched the pavement of Highway 85, staunchly declared that he had not crossed the road. Though they may have pirouetted or cartwheeled across, they had not crossed it - at least, not in his mind.

At the tender age of seven, it's easy to rationalize actions in one's head. Despite the dubious reasoning, the child was convinced they were 98% truthful. Their unblinking gaze met their mother's, but their conviction was about to face its sternest test. The mother threw down the ultimate challenge:

"Do you swear to God to let the devil take you tonight, that you did not cross the road?"

Now, our protagonist was in a quandary. Though they may have been technically truthful, they couldn't shake the niggling feeling that they had just told a big, fat lie. Nevertheless, they maintained their unblinking facade and gave the response that would seal their fate:

"No, Mom, I swear to God, let the devil take me tonight. I did not cross the road."

With that, their mother, a skeptic to the end, sent them to their room to ponder the gravity of the falsehood they had uttered. Most seven-year-olds hadn't robbed a bank and lied to their mothers about it; that typically came after one's eighth birthday. A self-satisfied giggle escaped him as he walked away, believing he had pulled off the greatest con of his young life.

He passed without incident the rest of the day, the afternoon fading into evening and bedtime creeping upon him. But a startling realization washed over him just before the lights went out. He had told his mother the biggest lie of his life, and suddenly, he was consumed by fear. Hours ticked by as he lay awake, eyes fixed on the window, expecting the moonlight to turn crimson and the king of hell's demons to descend and claim them for the realm of misery and suffering.

As he lay there, fear gnawing at his resolve, he noticed something eerie. Tapping. Tapping on their window. This was the final straw, the ultimate terror.

"Let me in," a deep, booming voice intoned, shaking the young penitent boy to the core. He fell to his knees in avid prayer, appealing to his Lord and Savior for the enteral fate of his very soul.

"I'm locked out of the house," said his father.
To this day, John Daniel avoids truckers and lying like the plague.

Ouija

In 1998, In the throes of adolescence, JD, son of John and Josie, enjoyed learning about the occult and the world of aliens, devouring books on the supernatural, aliens, and cryptid creatures. His family abounded with stories of strange happenings, but he had yet to have any personal experience of his own.

When he lived in North Dakota, he was transfixed by the story of an Ouija Board from a friend named Tracy Whiting. She said she and her sisters had one when they were little. As with all displaced toys, Tracy decided it was taking up precious real estate in the closet and tossed it out.

The next day, when packing away summer clothes, Tracy was surprised to see the Ouija board in the same spot it had occupied for years. Maybe she had just thought about throwing it, taking it outside, and placing it in the dumpster. When searching for a knit sweater the next week, she noticed where it sat. Tracy was so disturbed this time that she recruited her sisters. They took the board in the box. It came into the fire pit, and watched it burn to ash. Once the embers finally stopped glowing and died, they felt at ease. The following month, they discovered the board on the top shelf where all the games were kept. They finally decided to let it lie and never move it again. They left it in that very spot when they moved out of the house ten years later.

JD often wondered what had become of it. Had the new tenants found it and discovered its unexplainable homing powers? What else might happen in different circumstances? Years later, he stayed in Dever for the summer with his Aunt Mary Ann and her son Dimitris. He and D worked at the Rentzios family restaurant in the Cinderella City Mall. On his lunch break, he visited the Spencer Gifts store.

He walked in, amazed at the variety of nostalgic items the store sold. After perusing the rock 'n' roll merchandise and Spiderman tee shirts, he wandered over to the games section of the shop. There it was, after all his years of searching: an authentic Ouija board. He picked up the box and stared in wonder for a few minutes. Roused out of reverie by Dimitris calling, telling him it was time to go, he decided he must have it. He hurried to the counter and quickly purchased this doorway to the other side.

When he was home unpacking new school clothes and effects at summer's end, he took his prized possession out of the box and read the instructions. They stated not to use the board alone, so being one to follow the rules always, he put the Ouija board back in the box, which slipped his mind for a few months.

The school was busy with homework, wrestling practice, football games, band practice, and the social life of a junior in high school. One afternoon, after practicing the song "Highway to Hell" for the 30th time with his band, the bass player Todd made a statement.

"This is the week of All Hallows Eve. We should do something scary!" JD's thoughts went to the box of supernatural he had up in the closet to the left of where he sat on his drum throne.

"I have an idea," he said. Showing Todd and Ryan his new toy, they took the Ouija board to the Pioneer Cemetery in Park City, Montana, at dusk to see if they could summon souls from the afterlife.

They spent deliberation walking around, finding the spookiest spot, sat down, laid the board on their laps, and placed their fingers on the planchette. They waited. For two hours, nothing happened. Searching, they found a rusted fence encircling three plots, housing ancient headstones with worn photographs of people put to rest at the turn of the last century. The dates ranged from 1904 to 1920.

Hope renewed, and they sat at the gate. Set back up, they focused their minds on a summoning and patiently waited. After 20 minutes, they were hungry and gave up. Defeated, they went home.

They went into JD's house to find his mother was sitting waiting. She asked how the evening went, and they reported their defeat. She discouraged them from tampering with the supernatural. It could be dangerous. They kept quiet, thinking the opposite because having no experiences felt they lacked the excitement it could bring. A thought occurred to JD.

"Mom, will you try the Ouija Board with us?" he asked. His mother was sensitive. He knew she'd had several encounters with the dead throughout her life. Having seen ghosts, he thought it might be helpful if she participated.

Immediately, Ryan sat down on a chair opposite her and put the board on his lap with the planchette on top of the board with his fingers delicately placed on said planchette. She looked at the board and shook her head, indicating that she wanted nothing to do with this adventure.

He looked at his mother with pleading eyes and asked her to try it. When all three petitioned, shaking her head put her hands onto the board.

The room changed. Static electricity pulsed the air, raising their hair. The room darkened, and the air around grew dense.

Without warning, the planchette jerked, scraping across the board five inches before had even asked it a question. Ryan jumped, nearly leaping out of his skin.
"I can't do this!" Ryan said. Flapping his hands, he said felt a shock at his fingertips. JD's first and last attempt to play with an Ouija Board was this.

Guardian Angel on Ice

In the rolling hills of Hamilton, Montana, JD spent his summers under the watchful eyes of his grandparents, Aloysius (Ollie) and Dorothy Lorbiecke. Among the cherished memories, he held dear, rare moments when his stern grandfather would share tales of days gone by shone the brightest.

Ollie was a man of few words, a gruff figure who believed in the value of efficiency and practicality. Actions spoke louder than words, a philosophy he held close since his formative years and one he carried throughout his life. JD was seven when he first felt the weight of his grandfather's silent wisdom. His cousin, a crafty manipulator, dared him to slurp his Cream of Wheat in defiance of table manners. And, as children do, he obliged, slurping louder with each spoonful.

The following morning, over a breakfast of oatmeal, JD decided to school his grandfather the art of etiquette. He kindly asked him to cease his slurping. What followed was a gentle yet firm rebuke. A hand, calloused by years of labor, brushed against JD's cheek, a shocking warning delivered. With unwavering resolve, Ollie proclaimed, "I'll slurp my oatmeal any damn time I want to!" He punctuated this declaration, slurping even louder, drinking the remnants from the bowl. JD learned not to cross the unspoken boundaries of his grandfather's world that day.

As years passed, JD grew closer to the man of steel. On rare occasions, Old Man Ollie would unveil the layers of his past, which the boy treasured.

On one particular day, Ollie granted JD the unique privilege of hearing a sacred story from his youth when working at an ice skating rink in Orange County, California. Here, he first laid eyes on the woman who would become his beloved wife.

Ollie watched Dorothy glide effortlessly across the ice, her grace captivating his heart. He never approached her. She always skated alongside a strapping young man who he later discovered was her cousin. The ice beneath them held their secrets, their synchronized movements telling a silent story of their own.

One afternoon, as Ollie prepared for a break, he noticed a stranger in the stands. The man wore brand-new racing skates, the finest money could buy. Intrigued, Ollie approached, eager to learn more about the exceptional skates. What he heard left him stunned.

The conversation between Ollie and the mysterious man remained shrouded in secrecy. Yet, what remained most profound that he did share with the stranger was that he was his guardian angel. They conversed throughout his break, sharing words beyond human comprehension. As an enlightened Ollie rose to return to work, he hesitated, turning back one last time to ask how that man could possibly know these things about him, only to find the man had vanished.

Ollie was a man of unwavering truth, never one to spin fanciful tales. If he shared this encounter, it happened as surely as the earth revolved beneath the sky. In the twilight of his life, JD often remembered this story, a reminder that the world holds mysteries beyond understanding and that one is never truly alone amidst the vast expanse of existence.

Raven Child

While working in Texas, a coworker of JD's told him this tale one stormy evening in radiology. In 1992, Tausha, just a six-year-old girl, lived with a chilling secret. She would wake in the middle of the night to an unsettling sight – a mysterious little girl standing in her bedroom doorway. This prismatic visitor was unlike any ordinary child. She was dressed entirely in black with long, raven hair and had piercing green eyes that glowed like the Aurora Borealis.

The encounters with this figure terrified Tausha, and whenever the spectral child appeared, Tausha would remain petrified in her bed. She believed her life would be in jeopardy if she touched the ground. These nighttime visits happened without any discernible pattern or reason. Whenever she appeared, Tausha stayed in bed, hoping that ignoring the presence would make her disappear.

The visits always took place in the darkest hours of the night. As Tausha grew up, she discovered she could compel the spirit to depart by rolling over and returning to sleep. The mysterious visitor seemed to vanish for good when Tausha turned twelve.

Now an adult, Tausha has a son of her own. Strangely, her son refuses to sleep alone in that room. He has never explained why but adamantly refuses to let his brother sleep there. It's as if the room still harbors a lingering sense of unease from its spectral past, or maybe he, too, has been visited by the green-eyed girl.

Tuxedoed Intruder

As an adult, Tausha returned to her childhood home, unaware it was a hotbed of inexplicable occurrences. One evening, during a small family gathering, she left the bathroom and headed toward the backyard, where her husband and a family friend conversed. Before stepping out, she turned back to shut off the bathroom light.

Emerging from the dark hallway into the bright family room, I nearly ran into a towering stranger dressed in a tuxedo.

Startled, Tausha blurted, "What are you doing here?" To her astonishment, the sharp-dressed man dissipated, vanishing into thin air. Confused and shaken, Tausha heard her husband and friend talking outside. They were unaware. No one had seen the life-like apparition but her. The experience left her shaken and uncomfortable alone in the house of mysteries.

Guardian of the Shadows

JD was the youngest of Pedro and Dolores' children. An insidious malevolence threatened to engulf JD and his wife Lori in their new neighborhood. With an air of forbidding uncertainty, they had stepped into a place that was meant to be their haven but had unwittingly become a battleground of supernatural forces.

Each day, Emmitt, their German Shepherd, would gallantly meet Lori at the end of the driveway when she came home, a loyal protector ensuring her safe return. His paws whispered a solemn promise to guard the family against lurking peril. Yet, beneath this canine courage lay a grim reality. In the very heart of the household, a sinister cloud grew darker with every passing day.

Downstairs, the children huddled together, their innocent minds haunted by malignant notions while an icy fear settled deep within their souls. JD, ever vigilant, sensed an ever-increasing malice lurking in the shadows. A heavy dread settled upon him, chipping away at his determination to stay within the walls of this house. He was reluctant to embrace a home tainted by unseen evil wholly.

The growing hostility intensified. Shadowy figures materialized, lurking ominously at the foot of their beds, hollow eyes radiating malefic intent. Whispers of torment filled the air, taunting and tormenting the family members as they sought refuge in their dwelling. Emmitt remained an unwavering sentinel.

He bore the brunt of these sinister assaults with undaunted bravery, positioning himself between the malevolent entities and his beloved family. His barks and growls echoed through the halls, a defiant challenge to the dark forces that sought to break their spirits. In a shocking display of the supernatural, objects began to levitate and shatter, pictures were flung from the walls, and furniture rocked of its own accord. Yet, their steadfast canine companion stood firm, his fur bristling with protective determination.

As JD and Lori struggled with the increasingly sinister onslaught, they found solace in Emmitt's loyalty. Each day, his presence provided a ray of hope among encroaching darkness. After a time, the disturbance in the house quieted; however, Emmitt seemed changed. After speaking with a neighbor, they feared their once-noble guardian had descended into darkness on their behalf. JD's family sought answers. With a tremor in their voice, their neighbor confided a bone-chilling belief. The loyal dog had absorbed an evil spirit, now held captive within him. The ominous transformation progressed. Emmitt, a former guardian of their family's hearth, now exhibited behavior that made his family nervous.

Fierce and unprovoked growls punctured the air. He snapped at Lori's mother, causing them to isolate the dog from the family unless under close supervision. Then, the unthinkable occurred. In an act of unprovoked terror, he lunged at Lori's sister, teeth sinking into her arm, the malicious entity within him taking control.

Their hearts heavy with grief, the family confronted a painful choice. It was a decision born of love for their loyal companion, who had protected them all those years. With tear-filled eyes and heavy hearts, they released their beloved dog from the vicious grip that turned him into a monster.

In the aftermath, a heavy silence blanketed their home. The evil presence was eradicated, leaving behind a family shattered by the sacrifice of their heroic guardian. Even in the face of corruption, the memory of their loyal dog's unwavering devotion became a beacon of courage that illuminated their darkest hours. Though their scars ran deep, they vowed never to forget the selflessness of their protector, who had willingly borne the burden of evil to keep them safe.

Maria Dubois

A beautiful woman named Mary grew up and married Pete, the son of Pedro and Dolores. Mary herself rarely came to be because her father nearly died in infancy and again in childhood.

Mary's Father lost his mother, Estefana, succumbing to tuberculosis within two months of his birth in December 1930. Being ill during her pregnancy, she knew her son would struggle to survive and live a healthy life. Before she passed, she explicitly told her husband, whom she had selected to raise her infant. Maria Dubois, her closest cousin, who became known as Grandma Maria. She told stories of how sickly he had been as a baby.

She relayed a tale to us about her dad, at age 7, being under the weather. She awoke to him calling for her. When she entered his room, something she couldn't see but felt was there, an evil presence. Wailing, he clawed at the linens as it pulled him off and flipped him over to drag him under the bed. Grandma Maria grabbed him tightly as she vehemently prayed and demanded his release. After a bout of tug-of-war, the demon released him, and the boy was safe in the arms of his surrogate mother.

Maria said it only happened once. The family believes that Grandma Estefana chose Maria Dubois to raise her son because she knew that her child would one day need a prayer warrior to save him from whatever evil hoped to claim him. That little boy lived to be 89, passing gently of old age in 2020, surrounded by loving family laughing and spending time with him until the end.

Mary's father, content, wisely said, "If I have to go, I have to go." The family gave their final hugs and prayers, and within a half hour, he closed his eyes and was gone.

Eric Lingered

In the 1990s, during the August fair season, Mary Aguayo, wife of Pedro and Dolores's son Pete visited her friend Paulette in Baker, Montana. She was assigned to sleep in Paulette's son John's bedroom for the night. John was still in high school at this time. John was to sleep on the sofa in the living room. During the night, while she was asleep, John's best friend Eric, who was sleeping over, proceeded to lay over me thinking I was John and was saying,

"Get up, Man. Come on. Get up." He had been drinking and thought he was jokingly harassing John. When I realized he thought I was John, she told him.

"It's me, Mary. John is on the couch."
John woke up and yelled at Eric.

"I'm over here. Get over here." Eric felt so bad he couldn't apologize enough to Mary. He was so embarrassed. He went to John in the living room, still apologizing.

Eric was killed in an oilfield accident outside Baker a few years later. Being John's closest friend and like a son to Paulette, it left a wound in their hearts.

The next time Mary stayed at Paulette's, they were scheduled to go out of town together and drive the next day. She slept in John's old room as he was now graduated and not living at home anymore. During the night, Paulette woke her because she was tossing and turning, and Paulette could hear her from the bathroom and wanted to ensure she was alright.

The following day, Mary told Paulette that Eric had visited her in her sleep and reenacted the hilarious scene during the fair week years before. That's why she was tossing and turning. She felt something heavy on top of her and found herself trying to tell him it was me, not John, in the bed.

John grieved Eric tremendously, and Mary believed Eric's spirit stayed there because of the grief. She told Paulette about how her mom always told them about losing a brother and how deeply she felt loss. Her brother would appear to her every night, and she would tell Mary's dad every morning. Finally, her dad told her to pray for him and assure him she was alright so he could rest in peace.
At first, she didn't want to do it because she loved seeing him, but when she realized her husband was right, she prayed and started to release her grief, and he stopped coming to her. Whenever Mary stays at Paulette's, she always says a prayer to get a good night's sleep. If she falls asleep without praying, Eric wakes her and reminds her that she hasn't said her prayer yet.

Junior Boy

In 2014, Mary's brother Nick, Junior Boy, grew sick. She had been traveling with Paulette. After speaking with her dad and sister Nora, Mary made a quick trip home to Texas to visit him as his prognosis wasn't promising.

When she got there, Junior Boy reassured her, "I told you I was alright,"

She teased, "Too bad now you must put up with me." She took him to dialysis and chauffeured him around. The following day, they talked briefly before he went in for treatment. At this time, she felt she would never see him after this visit.

The next day, they went fishing in Victoria. He caught a big Red Fish and told his niece Melissa to take a picture and send it to Nora, telling her she missed out. He was a joker, which was his way of dealing with life. Within two weeks, Junior had passed away. The next time Mary saw him was for his burial. It was a devastating loss. She was thankful for listening to her intuition, which sent her home to spend time with him weeks prior.

Carolina Snow

While in Victoria in October 2014 for Junior's funeral, Mary's sister Carolina, heading to the funeral services, slipped and fell. She was taken by ambulance to the hospital. After Junior's burial, Mary went to the hospital to stay with her instead of to the funeral reception, even though she was leaving town shortly after.

While there with her, Carolina kept telling Mary, "Go be with everyone. You can't do anything for me here."

Mary responded, "I am not leaving you alone here, Carolina. I am staying until Nora gets here, and that's that." Carlina laughed despite being in pain, thankful for her sister's comforting support. They had to give her anesthesia and relocate her shoulder for her. Sitting there with her, Mary had the same feeling that she would not see her again.

By December 31, 2014, Carolina passed away two months after Junior. Mary didn't go to Victoria immediately as she would be cremated, and the services were not being held for a few weeks.

Pete and Mary were headed to the airport from Park City to pick up Kathy, their daughter, who was flying home to Billings. The Montana roads were icy and dangerous. Pete was driving with extra care that morning, carefully watching in all directions. Spotting a truck barreling behind them, Pete inched over to the shoulder to keep out of harm's way. They saw the car lose control and slide towards them just as it came alongside them. Somehow, just as it was about to make contact, with a crash and a bang, the truck shot over the road's median embedded in the snowbank on the opposite side of the intersection.

Pete started swearing as he pulled further onto the shoulder, saying, "I can't believe he hit us."

"No, he didn't," Mary told him.

"Didn't you feel the big thump against the truck?" Pete asked.

"You were driving. I watched the truck the whole time. I know he didn't hit us." Pete, cussing up a storm, examined their freshly repainted 2000 Ford F350 that had just been remade new inside and out. Any damage would have been easily spotted. Their truck was untouched. The other vehicle, stuck in the snow across the lanes, had been shot across the interaction. Pete climbed back inside, stunned to describe not a scratch.

Again, he asked, "Didn't you hear it?"

"No. The thump you heard was Carolina keeping us safe from a fatal accident and knocking that guy across the road." Unharmed, they picked up Kathy, thankful for another holiday, which was thanks to Caroline, Mary told her family and genuinely believed it.

Shotgun Shadow

Mary flew from Texas to New York City to meet Paulette, who was subletting an apartment in which they stayed when in the area. The apartment was laid out like a shotgun house in New Orleans, straight from front to back, with no doors except for the bathroom and entrance doors.

Mary was exhausted from travel. When she lay down, she slept deeply. Her bed was a convertible couch in the living room by the window. Asleep, Mary sensed a shadow advancing from the furthest point of the room, coming near. She felt it slide up the couch. Unafraid, she understood it wanted to leave the apartment. She unlatched the window and watched as it slipped up her hand and out. She believed the depth of her grief surrounding the loss of Junior Boy opened her up to what this spirit needed, making the experience possible.

Zariah's Angel

Mary's nephew Markie married a lovely girl named Jessica. They had two little girls while living in Victoria, Texas. It had been a few years since Mary's mother's passing in 1999. Jessica was driving with the girls through town when the six-year-old Zariah pointed toward the heavens. "Look, Mommy. There's Nana," Zariah and her younger sister were peering out the window, smiling and waving upward. Jessica looked but saw nothing unusual.

"See her, Mama? It's beautiful where Nana is. She's in the beauty! Do you see her, Mom?" Zariah asked excitedly. Jessica, tearing up, couldn't answer but smiled and said a prayer of thanks to the precious angels among them, sending love and keeping them safe.

Tank

Tank was Mary and Pete's Saint Bernard. He was a good boy who loved everyone. When they would go out of town, Marissa, their daughter-in-law, came over to take care of the dogs. When Tank was seven, Marissa watched the dogs play on the porch and saw rays of light bouncing off him. Finding it an interesting phenomenon, she snapped some photos. Tank had lived a healthy life. He had had some minor medical procedures, but nothing the vet couldn't easily address.

After Marissa took the pictures, his health declined. This time, the vet said Saint Bernard has the curse of all large breeds and is so big that their life expectancy can be as low as seven years. They'd given him a healthy, happy life but may lose him soon. Knowing their time was ending, they left the clinic somber.

On the way out, saw Tank with new eyes. He struggled to walk and could no longer jump in the car to accompany them on an adventure. Not wishing him to suffer, scheduled the appointment to put him to rest. The next day or two, Tank received extra treats, and the family spent time loving on him. After his passing, they were comforted with stories of him with the family and what a treasure he had been for the time they had him. These accounts demonstrate the powerfully comforting presence of the spirits of loved ones we've lost and how those whom we love, we never really lose.

Footfalls

In Mary Aguayo's home, many people had heard disembodied footsteps. Mary had heard footsteps upstairs when she was downstairs and footsteps on the small staircase when she was elsewhere and home alone. She used to think it was her dog, Payton, but he would lie right next to her every time she heard them.

When they stayed over, Mary and Pete's daughter Kathy had several experiences, as well as John and Josie. Mary's niece, Melissa, well informed of the activity, just spoke to it with no nonsense. She was sleeping one night when she began to be harassed, having her blankets tugged away. Too tired for games, put one fist in the air and said,

"I'm in no mood." Threatening, "I'll take you on!" The tugging stopped.

Come summer, Kruz, Makael, and Kaden, Mary's grandkids, slept over, as they often did. Pete had gotten up and left for Bozeman early that day. The youngest, Kruz, got up early and was outside riding the four-wheeler and playing with the dogs. Mary was working in the office downstairs when Makael and Kaden came down and sat at the island counter in the kitchen.

Makael asked, " Meemaw, where's Grandpa?"

Mary said, "Bozeman."

"Did he just leave?"

"No. He left before dawn this morning."

"Where's Kruz?"

"He's been riding the four-wheeler for an hour," she said. The boys looked at each other.

"Meemaw, something or someone slammed the door to our room upstairs." Skin prickling, Mary didn't want her sweet grandkids to be afraid in her home. So, she brushed it off.

"I don't think so. It may have been a breeze that shut it." They looked at each other.

"No. It didn't just shut," said Makael adamantly.

"It was a loud slam, Meemaw." Kaden chimed in. Mary just repeated that she didn't think it was anything, that there had to be an explanation. Trusting in the wisdom of their matriarch, relaxed.

"Maybe," The boys went on with their day unphased. Mary knew it was likely their friendly ghost, but she preferred not to frighten the children with the notion.

Payton Eternal

When Mary struggled with sleep apnea. Before receiving treatment, she was often lethargic during the day. She owned a bright little schnauzer named Payton, whom she referred to as her soulmate dog. Wherever Mary was, there, too, was Payton keeping watch. While out running errands, Mary felt especially tired. Payton whined while she drove, keeping her alert. While in the bank drive-through, she was in line with her foot on the brake, waiting.

She was roused from sleep by Payton scratching roughly at her hand on the gear shift. She had fallen asleep behind the wheel. Fortunately, she wasn't moving, but she would have likely wrecked if she hadn't been woken when she was. Little Payton woke her up, knowing something was not right. Constantly vigilant, he did well to keep her safe.

Mary and Pete had several dogs before, and Mary loved them all, but Payton was extraordinary. Everyone saw the unique bond the two shared.

    In his old age, Payton developed cancer. There came a time when it was inoperable, and the dog had little but suffering ahead, and Pete and Mary chose to say goodbye. The couple stood sentinel over him as the vet shaved his leg and injected him with heavy sedatives. He relaxed, growing sleepy. Mary gave him his final hugs and cuddles while he lay limp on the cold, sterile table. She wrapped his blanket around him tight as he huffed a last sigh. Mary wept as she felt him slip away. Thunder cracked, the heavens opened up, and it began to pour.

The drive home was quiet. Pete drove, holding Mary by the hand, tears falling. She knew it was the merciful and loving thing to do but wasn't ready to face moving on without her shadow. It was dark and rainy when they pulled in. Pete jumped out to ensure the material shed was locked. Mary, sniffling, pulled her jacket tight around her. Pete ran back to the car and opened the door in the gale.

"Honey, I just saw Payton in the driveway. It's okay. He's still here watching over you, and now he'll be young and spry forever." Mary smiled, knowing she still had the protective love of Payton, the angel dog.

Night Visitor

In a peaceful and hidden hamlet of Windsor, Idaho, cradled within the gentle arms of towering pine trees, a grand two-story residence crowned by a balcony sheltered the Villareal family. Terri and her family shared a haven, accommodating two other families in its warm embrace. The house sat at the end of a winding drive, surrounded by lush pine groves, cocooned by vast fields that whispered secrets to the wind.

Sun dipping below the horizon cast long shadows across the landscape. Terri and Shaddy enjoyed the comfort of their home. Tall pines swayed gently outside, their boughs rustling with secrets of the forest. Below, a quaint yard beckoned beyond which a steep embankment separated it from a swiftly flowing river.

On this particular evening, the men of the house had gone out earlier for a fishing expedition, and as the sky darkened, they returned bearing the fruits of their labor. The aroma of their catch still lingered in the air when something startling occurred.

Terri descended the staircase to join her husband and their companions—Hector, Shaddy, and Jimmy. The men had climbed the stairs to the upper floor, their laughter and camaraderie filling the room. With the arrival of Terri, the atmosphere shifted, and the joyous banter turned into hushed whispers of fear.

From the forest, a sound emerged, a fluttering of massive wings. Growing, the sound drew the attention of everyone. The men, gripped by terror, rushed back into the safety of the house, faces pale, scrambling for cover.

Terri stood transfixed. Her eyes locked on the shadowy figure outside. It was a bird unlike any she'd ever seen. Its enormous wings seemed to bend the sturdy pine tree, and its dark form defied the logic of the natural world.

Sensing her bold fascination, the colossal creature took flight, showing its complete form. It circled the house, its presence shrouded in the darkness of night. Cloaked, its wings whispered secrets as it soared, and then, as suddenly as it had arrived, it vanished into the inky abyss.

The men, still trembling from the encounter, dared not venture outside again after dark, especially not as far as the river. Terri, forever rapt by the memory of that visitor, would often gaze out into the forest, wondering about the strange creature that had descended upon their home. The pine trees, guardians of ancient obscurities, kept their knowledge hidden, and the Villareal family would forever be left with the memory of that mystifying flight.

Nocturnal Demon

In 1981, a modest house on Carmen Street burrowed in the projects of Victoria, Texas, held a family's hopes and dreams. Terri watched over her son, Mario, as he navigated childhood innocence. Little did she know that one night would bring an encounter that would imbed in their memories.

Terri's maternal instincts went on high alert one night as she noticed Mario frightened. The lively boy was cowering wide-eyed in terror, dread emanating from him. Terri's concern deepened as she pressed Mario to reveal the source of his fear. After hesitant silence, he found his trembling voice recounting the tale.

He described an enormous black bird, an evil presence that had descended upon him.

As Mario lay asleep, unaware of the impending terror, this ominous creature had landed upon him, its weight pressing down upon his small chest. The bird's sinister intent became apparent as it leaned over his mouth and stole his breath, shadowy wings wrapping tight around him like a suffocating shroud.

Awakening abruptly from this nightmare, Mario gasped for air, the specter of death looming perilously close. Barely escaping its clutches, his desperate cries for help pierced the veil between dreams and reality.

Terri listened awestruck to her son's chilling account. The menacing image of a monstrous bird descending upon her child chilled her. Her heart ached for her son, who endured this horrifying ordeal alone in the dark. Terri, overwhelmed with dread, recalled the event.

Their sanctuary harbored unspeakable darkness. She vowed to protect and shield her son from the evil forces threatening their peace. Though time would eventually fade the surreal memory, the hellion cast shadows over them. Terri and Mario learned the harsh reality that sometimes, fear could manifest itself in the most unexpected ways, blurring the boundaries between the known and the unknown.

Incubus of Utah

In the vast, rugged expanse of Utah, where deserts stretch endlessly beneath boundless skies, two young brothers, Terri's sons Mario and Oscar, four and six, had an encounter that impacted their young lives. The sun climbed high in the scorching desert sky. The boys were playing in the arid landscape near their home, boyish laughter echoing in the still landscape. Little did they know, their adventure would take a turn, plunging them into a world of suspense.

Frolicked, the brother's playful antics led them to an unassuming patch of land. Beneath the solid ground, something stirred. Without warning, the earth shifted, shuddering, creating a rift in the fabric of reality. A hole, abysmally black, opened up before bewildered eyes.

Three nightmarish figures emerged from the gaping maw of the chasm, forms twisted and grotesque. Glowing eyes with unholy malevolence reached toward the terrorized boys, skeletal fingers extending like claws.

Fear strangled Mario and Oscar, but they rallied. Relying on their youthful audacity, they fought back against the ghoulish assailants. Small fists landed with surprising force, connecting with the evil entities in a desperate bid for survival.

Their brave actions yielded a miraculous result. As the brothers struck the demonic creatures, a blinding light erupted from the earth.
After a harrowing battle, the grotesque goblins were consumed by the searing radiance, tortured wails fading into the ether. Just as suddenly as it had appeared, the gaping hole in the earth sealed itself shut, leaving no trace behind.

The desert landscape returned to its former stillness as if the skirmish had never occurred. For Mario and Oscar, there was no doubt it had been confirmed. Valiant hearts pounded with the remnants of fear and adrenaline. They clung to one another, seeking solace in the safety of their sibling. The memory of that day was a vivid reminder of the sinister forces that lurked beneath below. As the years passed, the brothers grew older. Still, the duel in the desert would remain fixed in their memories, a testament to the indomitable spirit of two young boys who had stared fear in the face and emerged victorious, their bond as brothers stronger than ever.

Lifesaving Elixir

Back in the 1960s, in the heart of Victoria, Texas, Alfredo Chavez had a steadfast routine. Every weekend, he'd attend dances, drink his fill, and sway to the rhythmic melodies of Vicente Fernández, Luis Miguel, and Javier Solís. Once tired, he would enjoy the long stroll home whistling the tunes, recreating whatever songs replayed in his mind.

The moon hung low in the star-studded sky as Alfred began his journey homeward. He strolled along the darkened pathway home with a bottle of whiskey clutched in hand. The sky was silent, save for the clatter of the railroad tracks wound through the town's outskirts.

Alfredo, stumbling parallel to the tracks, beheld a figure unlike any he had ever encountered. The mysterious silhouette was seated on the cold, unforgiving steel of the railroad tracks in a cloak that billowed like the tenebrous wings of a condor.

His mouth went dry as he cautiously approached the stranger. The shrouded man turned his head slowly, revealing naught but the hollow darkness of his hood. He requested a drink and a cigarette in a voice that seemed to emanate from a place of misery.

Fearful but morbidly curious, Alfredo extended the offerings to the vagrant. The shrouded man accepted the cigarette, placing it between his lips, and grasped the bottle with bony fingers. Alfredo's lighter sparked, casting a brief, flickering light upon the hooded face. He was met with a ghastly sight—a skeletal visage devoid of flesh, grinning maniacally from beneath the wicked hood.

Terror seized Alfred. Fleeing, he clutched his heart, footsteps pounding a frantic rhythm against the night. Stumbling and staggering, he did not dare look back until he reached home's safety.

The following days were torment. Agonizing abdominal pains, an intense fever, and paranoid delusions wracked Alfredo. Despairing, his wife Julia summoned a curandera, a healer of old-world wisdom. She uncovered the truth of his affliction with a knowing gaze by sharing his drink with the malevolent spirit on that cursed night. He had invited darkness into his very being.

The curandera crafted potent remedies and concoctions to soothe his ailing stomach and purge his mind of evil. As Alfred consumed the elixirs, he was overcome by violent convulsions. He retched and gagged, vomiting forth a vile, black mass consisting of twisted, knotted strands of hair and scabby pustules that bore the malignance that had seized his soul.

Once intertwined with his essence, the sinister spirit was violently expelled, leaving the desperate man in profound exhaustion. It was a purification unlike any other, a life-threatening ordeal that forever changed him. From that day onward, he swore off alcohol, forever haunted by the spectral encounter that had nearly cost him his life and soul.

Calling Collect

At age ten, JD's life took an unexpected turn when he was diagnosed with Type One diabetes. The symptoms were unmistakable: frequent urination, unquenchable thirst, and rapid weight loss. It was an alarming experience. He received the life-altering diagnosis in a doctor's office, a daunting 36 miles away from home. It was discovered that JD's blood sugar levels were dangerously high. He was concerned that JD could slip into a coma, with the grim possibility of renal failure. He was rushed to the hospital, where the medical team administered insulin to control his blood sugar levels.

The ordeal was excruciating, especially for a child terrified of needles, a fear that lingers to this day. JD's aversion to needles was so intense that, on one occasion, he eluded the doctor's injection by slipping behind his mother's chair and clinging tightly to her neck. The doctor eventually relented, sparing JD the needle but denying him the coveted sucker that usually followed such unpleasant experiences.

During the first two days of his hospital stay, JD's mother remained steadfast at his bedside, offering him comfort and reassurance. His father gently urged her to return home and get a shower and some much-needed rest. Reluctantly, she left after kissing her son and telling him she loved him, promising to return in the morning.

The terror JD experienced during those nights was beyond description, an emotion that had long since been buried beneath the passage of time. The medical staff gave him medication to help him fall asleep, as he was inconsolable. But after a couple of hours, he awoke, overwhelmed by fear, and desperately called out for his mother.

"Mom, I need you here, I'm scared," he pleaded.

He heard her gentle reply, "Get some sleep. I'm watching over you. I'll be back in the morning." He relaxed. "I love you," she told him.

Smiling, "Okay, Mom. I love you, too. I can't wait for you to get back." With that, he drifted off to sleep. True to her word, when JD awoke, his mother was seated in her familiar chair by his bedside.

His stomach rumbled with hunger. He expressed his gratitude while savoring his breakfast of cream of wheat and a single slice of toast.

"Thank you, Mom, for staying with me last night." Puzzled, she responded, "But, sweetie, I went home last night." Confusion clouded JD's face as he recounted their conversation, convinced it had been real.

"No, Mom, we talked last night," he insisted.

His mother smiled. "My God," she exclaimed, "I thought I had dreamt talking to you." With unwavering conviction.

JD assured her, "No, Mom, we did talk. I know because it was the conversation you remember having in your dreams."

Telekinesis Kid

AT twelve, living in Fairfield, North Dakota, JD eagerly anticipated two seasons each year: hunting and fishing. That year, John, his father, had secured Montana's deer hunting license and arranged with Aunt Judy to hunt on her property. The Burman ranch was renowned for its impressive deer with massive racks, and JD's father was on a mission to come home with a trophy buck.

Early Saturday morning, they set out. Eastern Montana and North Dakota autumn felt like winter, with a thick blanket of snow cover on the ground and nighttime temperatures plunging into the teens.

The men hunted tirelessly throughout the day while the ladies spent time at the ranch. However, as the sun began to dip below the horizon without a worthy buck in sight, John decided to call it a day, planning to return to the ranch in the morning to carry on.

Twelve-year-old JD, the excitement of the hunt mostly passed, wasn't thrilled about driving two hours back home, only to rise early and make the same journey back to his aunt's. Creatively, he mustered the courage to ask if he could spend the night there. Trusting his sister with his only son, John, set off back home, leaving JD behind.

Laying in an unfamiliar setting with strange noises and his mother so far away, homesickness washed over him. Panicked, he contemplated how he could have been traveling toward the comforting presence of home if only he'd ridden home with his parents. In his distress, he fervently prayed that he wouldn't have to endure the night without her. Then, as if by some miracle, his father reappeared in Aunt Judy's kitchen. His dad had barely been gone 30 minutes when he decided to turn back.

He relayed the strange turn of events to Uncle Marvin, explaining, "We got almost to the highway, and the lights went out on the truck." Secretly relieved, JD thanked the heavens for his good fortune. JD, his father, and Uncle Marvin went outside, where his dad pulled the truck into the garage with his mother still inside. They examined the truck's electrical system, and as mysteriously as the problem occurred, the lights flickered back to life. After a thorough inspection, they couldn't find any issue with the electrical system. JD piped up when it was time for JD's parents to head home again.

"You know," he told his dad, "I should probably go with you guys back home to get some rest, too. It will be a lot of work tomorrow hunting for that deer. Besides, if you lose your light again, you might need my help." His father gave him a knowing look, realizing that his son had lost his nerve. Without a second thought, John ushered JD into the passenger seat, where he sidled in next to his mother. Their '73 Chevy truck never experienced another electrical problem from that day forward.

Haunted Hunting Lodge

JD, John and Josie's son, and his wife, Marita, eventually left Roswell and relocated to Texas, where they'd often traveled to visit and attend conventions. Living in Texas made these adventures more convenient. When they lived in Roswell, their Texas travels would leave them getting home just in time to shower for work on Monday morning. One weekend, the couple was headed to Arlington from their West Texas. They left when JD came home from work Friday evening and drove until 2:00 am. Exhausted, only a few hours from their destination, they decided to rest at the next hotel rather than risk falling asleep at the wheel.

It was misting. The roads were slippery, and a thick fog had settled around them. They pulled into a dank, dark parking lot at an old hunting lodge with burned-out bulbs and a neon sign that advertised rooms for rent. A Kia pulled in just ahead of them. Two men parked and entered the front door. The lodge was less than inviting but seemed safer than the hazardous roads.

Marita found her shoes and gathered her purse while JD turned off the ignition and grabbed his wallet. They entered the foyer a few minutes behind their fellow travelers. There was a worn desk and a counter with a small coffee pot and Styrofoam cups. The walls were adorned with relics of the past. To the left were stairs leading to an upper story where the lodgers were to stay. The couple examines the authentic décor that could pass for an 1800s old-time saloon with the brothel on the floors above the bar. The clerk was nearly done checking in the passengers of the Kia. Handing them a key with a large plastic tag attached, she said, "Suite 10. That's a safe room." They looked at her questioningly but, shrugging, turned away, too tired to worry about what that could mean, and ascended the creaky staircase.

JD stepped up to the counter as Marita checked the map on her phone to see how much driving they would have in the morning. Buggered to see they had no service; she dropped her phone in her purse. Filling out the paperwork, she scribbled her autograph, not reading the fine print indicating that they would be responsible for repainting the entire building if they left a scratch.

Pushing her glasses up on her nose, the woman with a pilling sweater and lopsided bun handed them a key with a tag marked with a hashtag and the number fifteen.

JD, always the student, asked, "Is room fifteen safe, as well?" The clerk looked at him and turned around without a word, returning to her crossword puzzle. Amused at his antics, he picked up their duffle bag, and they trudged upstairs. At the landing, they turned right, entering a hallway of doors marked with a number.

After passing five rooms, they found fifteen at the end of the hall. As JD moved to put the key into the lock, they heard someone bustling around on the other side of the door. Husband and wife looked at each other. It seemed an odd time for housekeeping. It sounded like someone was trying to leave the room. Opening the door, they expected to come face to face with staff but were greeted only by darkness.

JD stepped in and found a lamp. Clicking the switch, nothing happened. In the dark, JD said he would talk to the clerk about the lights not working while Marita pushed past, looking for the restroom.

Seeing a door to the bathroom, entered and closed the door. Unafraid of the dark, sat down and answered nature's call. She felt about for the tissue. Flushed. Feeling for the soap, finding it next to the faucet, she washed her hands. She wiped her wet hands on her jeans and took cautious steps, feeling for the door handle. Marita opened the door and saw he had turned on the lamp by the door and the second across the room.

He was nowhere to be found. She looked out the window and saw him out by the vehicle, gathering their other bags. Looking around the room, she wrinkled her nose at the multiple beer cans crumpled up and stuffed in every place directly out of sight. She found one outlet near the door and plugged her phone into the charger.

Hearing the lock turn, she turned and saw JD coming in with bags on each shoulder and a light bulb in his hands.

"Oh! How did you turn the lights on?" He queried.

"What do you mean?" she asked.

"How did you turn the lights on? I went down to tell them they wouldn't turn on, and the old crab handed me a light bulb and said to change it myself." Not knowing her husband to be a prankster, she cracked a smile.

"Are you messing with me?" she asked, hands on hips.

"What?" he asked as he bustled past, setting down the heavy bags.

"I came out," pointing to the bathroom, "and they were on."

They stood looking at each other, speechless. Her stomach tightened as he grew suspicious of foul play. He remembered the sounds they heard before entering. He walked the room once, then twice, looking for hidden doorways or secret panels. Once reasonably satisfied there were none, they undressed and crawled into bed for a few hours of sleep. It wasn't long before JD snored gently, and Marita chided herself for being nervous and wasting precious rest. Just as she began to doze, the phone started making announcements at the peak volume as if someone was using Google Maps.

"No GPS Signal." Marita bolted upright, startled. She always kept her phone volume to silent or vibrate.

"Unable to Retrieve Map Data." It spoke as an afterthought. She looked at JD and, seeing him sleeping, got up. She crept across the room. As she neared the phone, it blared,

"Location Services Disabled." She hightailed it to the phone and turned the volume to silent. She closed the app and went to put her phone on Airplane Mode. She saw it already was, meaning it shouldn't be doing anything. She wrapped her arms around her as the cold seemed to embrace her. She adjusted the volume to silent and set it down quietly.

Tiptoeing back to bed, the phone blared, "No Internet Connection. Map App Crashed. Map Data Outdated. No Search Results Found." She hustled across the room and shut the device down.

She went back to bed and lay down. Lifting her husband's hand, crawled into his arms, resting her cheek on his chest. He sighed and patted her reassuringly.

She was nearly asleep when she heard a humming sound like an old refrigerator motor. Nothing was in the room but a bed, two nightstands, and two lamps. No TV or microwave. Nothing was capable of making any electrical humming. She ignored it but it grew louder. Just as she rolled over to wake her husband, it stopped. Later, she heard it again but, exhausted, put a pillow over her head and tried to continue sleeping.

She slept on and off until well after sunup. Marita, always the first to rise, gathered her toiletries and went to shower. Undressing, she turned on the water. The bathroom filled with steam. No matter which way she turned the knobs, it seemed the choices were scalding or even hotter than that. She had planned to wash her hair but couldn't bear it.

She stood outside the water flow and burned her palms, splashing water to damp herself. Before climbing out, she soaped up and splashed enough water to rinse off. Guessing the cold-water knob was broken, opened the bathroom door to release the steam so she could use the mirror. It seemed dangerous to have guests stay in a room where they were guaranteed to be burned. She put on her makeup and pulled up her hair. She went out into the room just as JD was waking up.

"Be careful with the hot water knob," she cautioned. "Feel the water before you get in." He grunted, not being a man of many words this time of the day. She set out his clothes and toothbrush and carried the other luggage downstairs.

When she came back, he was showered and scowling.

"No warm water at all?" he asked. She was stunned.

"You mean, only hot?" she clarified.

"It was ice. Nothing but ice," he said. They knew something strange was happening when she told him about her shower and the strange noises at night.

They went downstairs and were taken aback. The lodge had an entire gift shop attached to the lobby that neither had seen the night before. They recalled that they were looking at the wall with old memorabilia, a solid wall.

Entering the gift shop, the cheery woman behind the counter asked about their night. They confessed that it was odd. She wondered how so. When they described the events, she laughed. She explained that the lodge was haunted, but the ghosts in room fifteen were mischievous but harmless, unlike the poltergeists in room twenty-three. She said they only rented that room when the hotel was full. Perusing the shop, they listened to her tales of the spirits who haunted the hotel and how they came to be. A maid was killed in an accident just off the property and perpetually roamed the halls. Guests were murdered by a rifle in room twenty-three after a dispute broke out among hunters. The aged owner died of an aneurysm while changing light bulbs atop a ladder in room fifteen. They listened, intrigued.

The shop was filled with knick-knacks and other oddities. Marita asked from where they came. The woman told her this was practically a ghost town with the permanent residents passing on. The owner shopped estate sales. All these items were personal property of those who once lived in the village.

Finding it interesting, Marita purchased a glass vase with the cursive initials LBC. The woman wrapped it in tissue and wished them well on their travels. They left the hotel, and for the rest of the weekend, wherever they stayed, her showers were boiling hot while his were painfully cold. There was a slight concern that bringing that vase home might be a bad idea. It seemed a paranormal passenger traveled with them for the rest of the trip. Luckily, they were not followed all the way home.

Hunting ET

Living in Roswell, JD had the opportunity to interact with a diverse group of people, thanks to the town's enduring connection to the famed UFO crash of 1947. Many visitors worldwide flocked to Roswell in the hopes of glimpsing interplanetary beings. As it happened, JD had more encounters with illegal aliens than extraterrestrial ones.

One intriguing observation JD made when he first arrived in Roswell from Montana was the sentiment among the native residents. Many locals didn't support the hype that a UFO crashed into the desert on July 8, 1947. They believed that the widespread excitement about aliens resulted from the extravagant celebrations and publicity surrounding the 50th anniversary of the incident in 1997. However, his aunt Judy recalled hearing people discuss the event after it happened in the 1950s. This suggested there might have been more to the story than rumor.

Despite skepticism among Roswellians, JD remained compelled by the possibility of alien encounters and occasionally inquired with older residents if they had any tales from that era. Most of them dismissed his inquiries, insisting he was wasting his time. Reiterating the news announcement that the military had recovered a weather balloon. Nevertheless, JD's persistence paid off, leading him to a gentleman who witnessed peculiar activity that summer. According to the man's account, he had been out rabbit hunting with friends on Pine Lodge Road, a few miles east of town. A hot evening morphed into a raging lightning storm illuminating a black sky. The dry summer heat heightened electrical activity. He and his buddies were driving when he noticed a "silver, cigar-shaped saucer flying alongside his truck" just beyond the neighbor's fence. Both the car and the unidentified object were moving at a speed of about 35 miles per hour.

Startled, he leaped out of the truck with his rifle in hand, the .22 caliber weapon resting on his lap with its barrel pointed out of the window—just in case he spotted a rabbit. Shocked, he tumbled head over heels down the road while the truck continued to travel at 35 mph.

Tucking and rolling, he regained his footing. Jumping up, he aimed his rifle at the craft. As soon as he did, the UFO swiftly veered away, disappearing beyond the horizon before he could line up a shot.

Retraced his steps to the truck, which had stopped further down the road. He had quite a story to share when he rejoined his disgruntled friends inside the vehicle. Thankfully, despite his erratic behavior, no one was injured during this astonishing encounter.

The Brave Little Saucer

JD had an encounter with a woman who shared a story about an incident from her childhood. Her father was stationed at Walker Air Force Base in Roswell when she was four. Initially established in 1941 as an Army Air Corps flying school. During World War II and the postwar era, it was known as Roswell Army Air Field (RAAF) and remained active until its closure on June 30, 1967. Holding a position as an officer, the family resided in the expansive housing facility located on the north side of the base, designated for the families of military personnel.

One scorching afternoon on July 8, 1947, the girl and her mother sought refuge from the heat under the covered porch. They watched her father and brother playing basketball in the backyard from this vantage point. Sweltering, electrical storms had been lighting up the sky with streaks of lightning for hours. Unexpectedly, her father and brother abruptly ceased their game, gazing skyward. Her father gestured for her and her mother to come and see. Walking over to where they stood, directed their eyes upward.

To their astonishment, they witnessed an extraordinary sight—five saucer-shaped craft arranged in a V formation gliding through the sky. The inhuman vessels flew remarkably low, one hundred feet above ground, soundlessly. Absolutely soundlessly.

Watching, it became evident that one of the saucers at the end of the formation was experiencing some damage, causing it to wobble. Regardless, they all remained utterly silent. The enigmatic convoy of saucers vanished from their sight, with the last UFO continuing to exhibit signs of distress as it disappeared into the distance. This extraordinary sighting left an indelible impression on the girl and her family, an interesting addition to the anecdotal history of Roswell's mystique.

Lead Caskets

During another of JD's interviews, the proprietor of Ballard Funeral Home informed him that he'd taken ownership from its founding owner in the 1960s. He explained the discussion became interesting during the transition as peculiar occurrences were mentioned. The original owner recounted a bizarre order that had come through in July 1947.

A classified special order for caskets originated from Walker Air Force Base, marking it as a mysterious request. It involved the procurement of three child-sized coffins, each meticulously lined with lead and equipped with multiple locking apparatus, and, per the United States Government, were to be delivered to the base as soon as possible. The curious nature of this order left both Mr. Ballard and the former owner pondering its significance. The question loomed: What could have prompted the military to commission such an order? The eerie history of Roswell continued to unveil its secrets, leaving JD with more questions than answers.

Grays

JD had the additional privilege of conversing with a woman whose memories unveiled a secret surrounding a remote ranch in Corona, New Mexico, the established crash site. She recounted her days as a ranch worker during the sweltering summer of 1947. Her recollection was captivating. This was what she shared.

The sun's scorching rays bore down on the vast expanse, creating shimmering waves of heat licking the landscape. She knew something crashed on the property, an event that bewildered the military, unable to decipher the species that had visited. Diligently tending to her work tasks, she was drawn to the partially open door of the ranch owner's private office, a space generally locked and closed.

Stepping cautiously into the room, her senses immediately absorbed its atmosphere. The air was heavy with the scent of aged wood and leather-bound books, giving the office an air of historical prestige. The dim, dappled sunlight filtering through the curtains cast intricate patterns of light and shadow across the room. Her attention, piqued, crept further inside.

Within a moment, the ranch owner's wife appeared sternly, warning her of the gravity of her trespass. The housekeeper was promptly ushered out of the room, her heart racing as she contemplated the mysteries hidden within. Noticing an array of photographs on the ranch owner's desk, each carefully arranged. Turning back, she took a peek. She recalls they were of a damaged aircraft that had crashed and one of a small grey corpse. Thinking back, she now contemplates the value of those photos today.

Another memory resurfaced—a moment when she had been near the entrance of the ranch house. Through the door, she overheard the ranch owner engaged in a cryptic conversation with his hired hand. Their voices were hushed, veiling their words in secrecy.

"They are Native American pictograph symbols, is what we are going to tell anyone that asks," the ranch owner had uttered in hushed tones. Perplexed. She soon overheard one phone call scheduling a meeting with a government man. She was given an impromptu unpaid day off work the day of. She was surprised to receive a wildly generous Christmas bonus that year. It was the first and only one she received.

A transformation swept across the ranch in less than a year. The decrepit, worn-out equipment that had once dotted the landscape had vanished, replaced by a fleet of state-of-the-art machinery. It was as though the ranch had a very lucrative secret they had monetized. Early the next spring, she was dismissed from her post and a team of brainless young housemaids replaced her. The echoes of that mysterious summer still resonate in her memory, another fiber in the tapestry of Roswell's colorful history.

Supersonic Orbs

An ordinary evening in Roswell turned extraordinary as Marita, her friend Michaela, and their children embarked on a routine pizza run. With dusk falling, they cruised westward along McGaffey Road, heading back to Michaela's house. Suddenly, a small, luminous orb-like object streaked silently past their vehicle, hovering level with the passenger window. A shared look between the two women confirmed that they had both witnessed the curiosity. The enigmatic orb had traversed an impressive distance in the blink of an eye, darting far ahead on the road.

Instead of turning into Michaela's neighborhood as planned, an unspoken curiosity led them to continue west down McGaffey, determined to pursue the object. The orb remained visible to the west as they ventured farther, following its trajectory. They eventually reached the Relief Route, still within sight of the enigmatic orb.

Opting to continue their pursuit, they followed the Relief Route north until it merged with the highway, allowing them to continue their westward journey. As they approached the object, it appeared to hover motionless, teasing them with its elusive presence.

They maintained a speed of 60 miles per hour for twenty minutes, gradually closing in. A second orb materialized from the opposite direction, hurtling through the sky at an astonishing velocity. In the blink of an eye, these two celestial travelers, one originating from the north and the other from the south, converged and froze close to one another.

A few suspenseful seconds passed before both orbs, defying the laws of physics, darted off in opposite directions at speeds imperceptible to the naked eye.
Their display of agility and velocity left the witnesses in awe. The orbs vanished from view, leaving a lingering sense of wonder and a sky devoid of answers.

Marita and Michaela continued their journey, eyes trained on the heavens, but saw nothing else. Eventually, they turned back, retracing their path, gaze fixed firmly on the sky. However, the celestial visitors had vanished without a trace, leaving them to ponder these astonishing orbs' inexplicable origin and purpose, a mystery that remains unsolved today.

Anton Part Deux

When Marita's son Anton, a three-year-old on the autism spectrum, was young, he was selectively mute. Although he could, he rarely chose to speak. Not unlike many others, it was a Saturday afternoon when his mom, Marita, and his sister, Emmie, were spending time at a friend's house. At this house lived Michaela, her partner Bobby, and her two girls, Stephanie and Samantha. The girls were aged five to eight. Bobby was a stout, boisterous man who was always full of jokes and kept the kids laughing.

This afternoon, the mothers laughed as they watched Bobby being attacked by the three girls from all sides as he artfully slayed them. They jumped on his back and bear-hugged his legs in an attempt to slay the giant, squealing and laughing wildly. Bobby plucked them from his shoulders, gently tossing them onto the couch, only to be scaled again once their laughing fits subsided.

Not a big proponent of touching or interactive play, Anton watched out of the corner of his eye from the table with mildly amused approval as he replicated the match with the two figures he had in his hands.

He would smirk when he suspected his favorite, the eldest of the girls, Stephanie, might have gotten one over on Bobby and stifled a laugh as she was toppled down from her position.

During this particular bout, Anton suddenly got up from his game of solitude and stomped toward Bobby with his tiny fists balled up, arms held rigid and stared intensely at the man with narrowed eyes. Taken aback at this rare show of attention, Bobby feigned defeat and fell back on the couch, careful not to crush Emmie clinging like a marmoset while on his great descent.

"What's up, Anton?" Bobby inquired in surprise.

"I used to be great and big," Anton enunciated clearly. The room grew quiet as everyone tuned in to hear Anton's declaration. "-back before this, in the old days, when I was a man." Bobby swallowed, unsure what to say as these were the first words Anton had ever spoken to Bobby. The adults all looked at each other, perplexed. The girls stayed quiet, struggling to grasp what this could mean. Anton's mom approached him.

"What do you mean, Son?" but Anton, the moment having passed, chose not to answer, returned to his game, and never spoke of the memory again. The whole room, except for Anton, burst into animated discussion about what this meant. Each shared their theories on how this could explain so much about Anton's mysterious personality. Still, definitive conclusions remained unmade because the statement was destined to stand alone without elaboration or explanation.

It remained a mystery. Curiously, last month, his mother was reviewing the family books of genealogy and was confounded when she found the birth and death certificates of an Anton, who had lived and died about 100 years before her son Anton was born. It was an interesting discovery in their family's history. She had no idea he had a predecessor. It made her recall why she gave him that name when he was born. She remembered hearing it somewhere in a distant memory and tucking it away but couldn't say exactly when or why.

Time Loop

Living in Roswell, New Mexico, Marita spent much of her time traveling, bumping down nondescript country highways. On this occasion, her mother-in-law, Josie, was coming down to visit the family: her son, JD, his wife, Marita, and the two youngest kids, Emmie and Anton. JD had to work, but Marita and the kids made the three-hour trek from Roswell to Albuquerque to pick up Josie from the Albuquerque International Sunport, where she flew from Montana.

It was assumed that Josie might want to spend the day in the city shopping or dining before heading home. They weren't expected home until after dinner. Her flight arrived midafternoon. Marita and the kids had left home around 10:30 am to be sure to pick her up by 2:00 pm. It was hot, and Josie was already worn out from her day of travel. She was interested in getting home to rest.

They left Albuquerque and got straight on the road. The kids were hungry. So, they pulled off the highway in a small town called Edgewood, took a five-minute detour to get drive-through food, and ate on the road. The party continued east and hit their first landmark in about half an hour, right on schedule. There was a truck stop with a gift shop, and it was the only turn from Albuquerque to Roswell.

At Cline's Corner, they turned south and continued. From here, you'd drive an hour straight through one little gas station town called Vaughn and stay straight for another hour until you hit the Roswell city limits.

From the Cline's Corner turn, you could set a stopwatch for 2 hours, drive straight, and cruise at the speed limit, and in 1 hour and fifty-nine minutes, you'd be hitting city limits. She looked at her watch at the turn and saw that the time was 3:17 pm. The weather was sunny, the roads were clear, and the cruise control was locked.

The women chitchatted pleasantly as the afternoon passed, occasionally seeing a car or two traversing the opposite way.

After an hour and a half of steady driving with no oncoming traffic and no sighting of Vaughn, Josie began asking how much further they had to go. Checking the time, Marita admitted they should have hit Vaughn by now. They began to discuss the possibility of the driver making a wrong turn. Marita, having made this drive upwards of twenty-five times, assured her passenger that coming from Albuquerque to Vaughn, there was only one turn, right, at Cline's Corners. Emotions began to run high as they drove on, never reaching their destination. The kids were getting cranky. The hour grew later and later.

"Ah, poor kitty," Josie commented, seeing a cat on the side of the road in the grass.

"I didn't see it, but people abandon many animals around Vaughn. We're getting close." Marita replied. They drove on, and the road just seemed to lay ahead forever. After another hour passed, JD called. Home from work, he wondered if they were having fun in the city. Marita told him they'd headed straight home but had yet to hit Vaughn. Confused, he asked the time they left Albuquerque. Right at two, she clarified.

"You should be home by now," he told her.

"Another cat," Josie said.

"And some jerk abandoned a group of kittens out here," Marita said.

"No kittens!" her husband teased. "Do not bring home any more cats." She smiled.

"We haven't even stopped," she assured him.

"Where did you have lunch?" he asked.

"We got drive-through in Edgewood," she explained.

"We didn't even get out," his mother supplied from the passenger seat, now rubbing her stiff legs.

"Did you turn at Cline's Corners?" he asked, perplexed.

"Of course. Right. Just like always," she said. "And there's another solid black cat. That one looked exactly like the last one." Marita remarked, troubled.

"She took a wrong turn." Josie said loud enough for her son to hear on the other end of the line."

"Ma, there's no wrong turn. If she turned right at Cline's Corner, that's a no-brainer." Her son reassured her.

"Are we lost?" Emmie asked from the back seat. Anton contributed to the conversation by sleeping deeply, his mouth wide open and snorting as her mother patted Emmie reassuringly.

"No, Honey. We'll be in Vaugn anytime," her mother reassured her.

"Well, this is odd," JD remarked from home.

"Yes. Very," his wife agreed.

Within the regular time from there, they reached Roswell. None of them could explain the missing time or how they could have arrived in Vaughn if she had made a wrong turn. They would have inevitably ended up somewhere else if she had missed the proper turn. Some have theorized they were abducted by aliens and had their memories slated clean. They were in agreement that if something of that nature did occur, they would prefer not to remember and instead have the nagging feeling that something mysterious happened.

Over eight hours, the four appeared to travel the same stretch of road with no oncoming traffic, passing the same black cat repeatedly. Eventually, around eleven-thirty at night, they hit Vaughn. They stopped for a desperately needed bathroom break and stretched their legs. Unable to shake the feeling that they had been stuck in a time loop and not wanting to fall back in, they gassed up and quickly got back on the road. The two women discussed how if they were to have traveled the distance, they would have covered driving 8 hours, they would have run out of gas long before, and yet she'd pulled in with over a quarter of a tank

Phantom of the Wigwam

Marita was a professional dancer and exotic animal handler best known for belly dance, flamenco, and snake dancing, where she would perform intricate and unique dances, sometimes while balancing swords, flames, and other times adorned with pythons. In 2010, she and her dance partner were invited to perform at the Wigwam Cultural Museum for a Dia De Los Muertos festival in early November.

The Wigwam Museum, located at 110 E San Antonio Ave, is the headquarters of the Paranormal Society. Guests can browse artifacts collected through the years found in the building built in the 1800s. The Wigwam is documented as being the first saloon with electricity in El Paso, Texas. The earliest records say it was a gambling hall, brothel, and tavern owned by John Wesley Hardin, one of the most notorious pistoleros of the day. The building is well known to be haunted by the many people who died untimely passings there.

A small group consisting of Marita, her husband, JD, and two youngest kids, Emmie and Anton, Alice and her husband, Matt, as well as a student dancer, all traveled to the event together along with a few of her prized snakes. They arrived midafternoon, leaving time to peruse the festival. They were amazed by the art installations and relics on display and for sale in the Wigwam. They were shown a brief tour of the basement, littered with artifacts of yesteryear, and all felt strongly of unsettled spirits and times long gone.

There was a burgundy coffin lined with plush satin behind a velveteen rope, devilish art on display, and beautiful paintings lit by flickering candlelight. Marita and Emmie stood goosebumped as they listened to animated telling by a spooky narrator of the tragic tale of La Llorona.

In the depths of a moonless night, the tale of La Llorona unfolded when the air was heavy with the weight of forgotten sins and the river whispered secrets of centuries past. It was a tale to chill the bravest of souls and make the most hardened skeptic shiver.

Long ago, a woman named Maria lived in a small Mexican village among the devastating beauty of the Sierra Madre Mountains. Maria was said to be the most enchanting creature ever to walk the earth. Her long, obsidian hair cascaded like a waterfall. Her eyes, deep as the abyss, held a mysterious allure that could ensnare the hearts of men.

Maria's beauty, however, was overshadowed by her tragic fate. She fell deeply in love with a handsome ranchero, a man named Carlos, who had wealth and charm that rivaled her beauty. They were wed in a ceremony that seemed blessed by the heavens and soon after were gifted with two beautiful children.

As time passed, Carlos grew distant. His gaze wandered to other women, and his heart strayed from Maria's side. Consumed by jealousy and despair, Maria's love transformed into a gnawing obsession. She could not bear the thought of Carlos being in anyone else's arms.

One evening, in the grip of madness, Maria took her children down to the banks of the coursing river that flowed near their village. She drowned her innocent children in a rage and despair, their cries echoing through the night like mournful wails. Realizing the enormity of her crime, Maria, too, plunged into the cold waters, succumbing to the darkness that overtook her soul.

As she met her watery grave, a curse was said to have been cast upon her. Maria's spirit was doomed to wander the earth for all eternity, searching for her lost children, weeping for their souls. She became known as La Llorona, the weeping woman.

Those who have encountered her tell of a ghastly sight—a woman draped in a tattered white gown, her hair matted and dripping, her eyes hollow and filled with endless sorrow. She is said to roam the riverbanks and haunted pathways, her mournful cries echoing through the night. Some claim that her screams can especially be heard on a moonless night, echoing through the mountains, chilling the hearts of those who dare to listen.

But beware, for La Llorona is not just a forlorn spirit. She is a vengeful specter, known to snatch away wandering children, mistaking them for her own. She is said to reach out from the depths of the dark river, her icy grip pulling unsuspecting souls into a watery grave. To this day, the tale of La Llorona serves as a frightening reminder of the consequences of jealousy and obsession. As the night descends and the river's whispers grow louder, beware the weeping woman, for her mournful cries may be closer than you think, and her curse lingers in the darkest corners of the world, waiting to claim those who dare to cross her path.

Mother and daughter gazed at the melancholy artwork of the forlorn ghost, thanked the narrator for his moving telling of the tale, and went on their way. They stopped at several vendors and visited with other guests. As time for their performance neared, the women dressed for the show. JD prepared the snakes.

The women danced, entrancing their audience with their beautiful serpentine movements, sometimes in perfect sync, other times mirroring each other as the melody crescendoed, breaking into hypnotizing solos ending in perfectly practiced poses. The crowd broke from their hypnotized awe when their performance was over and applauded wildly. The ladies bowed graciously and left the stage to be crowded by excited fans asking for photos with questions about their dancing practices, Alice's dance studio, and their snakes. The ladies had their pictures taken and answered questions graciously until the crowd dissipated. By this time, the party was starving and ready to sup. With costumes and snakes packed away, Emmie and Marita took one more round of the booths.

"Mom, let me take your picture." Emmie offered, directing Marita to stand before one of the ghostly paintings. Marita posed in her sugar skull makeup. Emmie held up her camera. Marita looked over her shoulder. She thought she saw someone behind her. When she turned, all she saw was the painting. Turning forward again, she smiled. Emmie snapped the picture.

"It's pretty creepy here." Emmie shivered.

"It's said to be haunted," Marita told her daughter. The two gathered up their bags to join the rest of the party. The travelers found a phenomenal restaurant just around the corner and talked excitedly about the spooky atmosphere of the venue and the amazing event. The friends enjoyed spicy cuisine accompanied by tall, tangy margaritas. They gabbed about how their performance had gone so well, but what they remembered most was the heavy, intense atmosphere of the museum. It felt saturated with spirits, they all agreed. Emmie showed her mother the photo she had taken.

"Wow! You captured all the brilliant colors even in the dark setting." Marita remarked, smiling. Emmie passed the camera around to show the others the photo.

"Let me see that again," Matt said, pulling the camera back. "Who's your friend?" he asked Marita. Puzzled. She looked at the photo where Matt pointed. She swallowed hard as she noticed the dark shadow looming over her in the picture, appearing to lean on her with one dark arm draped heavily over her shoulder. Everyone passed the camera around. When the photo was printed, it was difficult to see, but if you look carefully, you can still see the spirit, which was enamored with the beautiful belly dancer with golden snakes.

Fanboy Everlasting

In 2014, Marita, a model, had a photoshoot scheduled down in a wooded area in Roswell. There was some disagreement over where the shoot would be held. Because it was sheltered, it was known for vagrants camping there. After an unseasonably cold autumn night, a man had frozen to death. After some discussion, the decision was made to shoot there. The model, her many costumes, and snakes arrived, joined by the photographers and armloads of equipment. Hundreds of photos were taken from all angles until sundown. The shoot was a success. The team said goodnight and went home.

It wasn't until a few days later, when Marita was reviewing some of the photographs from her desktop at home, that anything peculiar was noticed. Many photos were taken in a series as she moved to capture her movements best. In one pose, a shadowy figure in the trees seemed to run past. In one photo, the shadow blended in with the other shadows from the trees. It wasn't until you played them in a progression that the figure of a man appeared to be running behind her. The photos were passed from one photographer to the other. They all discussed what it could be. No one in front of her could have cast that shadow. The figure ran through the frame for three or four seconds and then vanished. Since you can't spot the shadowy figure unless you watch their progression, the husband and wife made a YouTube video showing the footage of the camera-shy phantom. Viewers remarked in the comment section that it was the most interesting case of photobombing ever, to which the model agreed.

Conclusion

In the closing chapter of this remarkable journey through the unknown, the reader stands on the precipice of human understanding, gazing out into the boundless mysteries of the universe.

Throughout the anthology, the narratives have traversed the realms of extraterrestrial sightings, where the heavens themselves have opened up to reveal enigmatic crafts and beings from beyond the stars. Cryptids have emerged from the shadows, challenging the perception of reality with their elusive existence. Ghosts and spirits have walked among humans, whispering secrets from beyond the veil of death.

The anthology has illuminated ritual séances that beckon the supernatural, Bigfoot and Chupacabra lurking in the shadows, and aliens whose motives remain shrouded in cosmic ambiguity. The extraordinary landscapes of sleep paralysis blurred the line between dream and reality, and astral projection carried readers to dimensions beyond the physical. Hauntings have reminded us that the past lingers in the present, and reincarnation unveiled the eternal cycle of life and rebirth.

Throughout this incredible odyssey, esoteric knowledge challenged conventional wisdom, inviting exploration and questioning of the fabric of reality. The anthology also showcased the extraordinary power of human love, bravery, and inquisition, which conquered the darkest mysteries and illuminated the path to understanding.

As the readers take their leave from these astonishing chronicles, they are reminded that the pursuit of the unknown is a testament to the indomitable spirit of humanity. In the face of the inexplicable, humanity has shown resilience, curiosity, and a hunger for knowledge that knows no bounds. Through these stories, the vastness of the universe, the intricacies of existence, and the limitless potential of the human spirit have been revealed.

The author expresses her deepest gratitude to the courageous and open-hearted members of the Aguayo and Lorbiecke families and the family friends, the guardians of their ancestral tales. Their willingness to share these accounts of magic and woe passed down through five generations has allowed readers to glimpse into the hidden corners of existence. With unwavering candor, they recounted their experiences with extraterrestrials, cryptids, ghosts, spirits, and the unfathomable forces that have shaped their lives. Their collective voice has breathed life into this book, and the author is profoundly thankful for that.

Marita Christine Lorbiecke extends her heartfelt appreciation to each real-life character in this book, from the long-passed patriarch, Gabriel, to the youngest of his descendants. Their willingness to reveal their lives' most intimate and extraordinary moments has illuminated the pages. Their stories have left an indelible mark on readers' hearts, reminding them of the limitless mysteries surrounding us.

It was the profound pleasure of the author who meticulously compiled and composed these tales into this grand tapestry. Her dedication to preserving these narratives, bringing legacy and life to these tales, and her artistry for storytelling have allowed the public to embark on this remarkable journey. Her words have breathed life into the unexplained and conveyed that the depth of human experience is extraordinary.

In conclusion, as readers reflect upon the profound significance of the stories shared within these pages, they are reminded that shared humanity unites us in the face of the mystery. These stories inspire us to approach the inquiries of existence with curiosity, courage, and an unyielding desire for knowledge. In closing, may the tales within these pages serve as an enduring testament to the resilience of the human spirit and the boundless nature of the quest for understanding. Together, readers have explored the realms of the extraordinary, and in doing so, they have enriched their own lives and expanded their collective consciousness. Let these stories be a beacon of inspiration, a celebration of the enigmatic, and a reminder that the quest for truth knows no bounds in the vast canvas of existence.

About the Author

Marita Christine Lorbiecke is an award-winning American author raised in the company of books, primarily through her mother, an avid lover of books, a philanthropist, and somewhat of an animal whisperer, which Marita inherited. Her first full-length novel was honored with the Literary Titan award for expertly delivering complex and thought-provoking concepts.

The ease with which she expresses the ideas conveyed reflects the author's talent in exercising fluent, powerful, and appropriate language. Growing up in nature, she became enamored with animals of all kinds and married and had children within a menagerie of exotic animals. To this day, Marita and her husband live on a seven-acre farm and own a private zoo that features hundreds of beautiful birds, giant tortoises and lizards, massive snakes, marsupials, and miniature livestock. She is a veteran educator in public schools as well as online. Marita attended college in New Mexico, earning several degrees, accolading a Master's degree. She works as a professional belly dancer, model, and snake wrangler in her spare time. She loves books, nature, and animals and has a passion for the art of language as a poet, children's author, and an award-winning international novelist.

EPIGRAPH

Whispers of Enchantment

In pages bound with dreams, my tales take flight,
An anthology that weaves the mystic thread,
Where words and worlds in harmony unite,
And realms unknown in whispered secrets spread.

Each poem and story, like a star's soft glow,
Illuminates the vast expanse of thought,
A treasure trove of feelings ebb and flow,
In melodies of prose and verse, love sought.

Through every page, enchantment's spell is cast,
A tapestry of magic, bright and bold,
The wonders of imagination held fast,
In tales of courage, love, and legends told.

With love my storybook, the magic thrives,
In every word, a universe survives.

-MC Lorbiecke

Μαριτα Χηριστινε Λορβιεχκε

www.ingramcontent.com/pod-product-compliance
Lightning Source LLC
Chambersburg PA
CBHW020633230426
43665CB00008B/153